THE FINANCIAL INGREDIENT
in Foodservice Management

John L. Bolhuis, Roger K. Wolff
and the Editors of NIFI

THE FINANCIAL INGREDIENT
in Foodservice Management

A NIFI Textbook

Published by D. C. Heath and Company
in cooperation with
The National Institute for the Foodservice Industry

Illustrations by Jack Stockman

Other textbooks in the NIFI series:

Applied Foodservice Sanitation
developed in collaboration with
the National Sanitation Foundation

Management By Menu
by Lendal H. Kotschevar

Published simultaneously in Canada.

Printed in the United States of America.

International Standard Book Number: 0-669-00009-4

Library of Congress Catalog Card Number: 76-9243

On behalf of the
people in our industry
who will benefit, the Institute
is pleased to thank
GENERAL FOODS CORPORATION
for the financial support
which has made possible the
development of this book and
related course materials.

Foreword

No restaurant or other foodservice operation can long survive, much less prosper, without sound financial management. And no foodservice manager can succeed in his job or grow to full stature in his profession without a firm grasp of financial principles and techniques.

As our country moves into her third century of nationhood, the foodservice industry accounts for more than five percent of the gross national product, and stands first of all industries in the number of its business establishments and the size of its work force.

But our fast-growing industry is also a highly competitive one. In the real world of operating challenges, dollar planning and dollar watching are absolute essentials for the men and women managing it. Inflationary pressures and big-government regulations have further increased the controls necessary to keep costs in line and attain a reasonable return on capital invested.

This book and associated courses, in the making for almost five years, have been designed to help managers make successful financial decisions. They provide a myriad of facts to guide the restaurateur in preserving the profitability of his business, and the institutional manager in holding to his budget—always with the ultimate object of quality service to their customers. Experienced managers as well as students will find valuable information on budgeting, cost control, and interpretation of financial records, presented in language that can be understood regardless of prior accounting experience.

I join the directors of our Institute in the hope that all who give these fine publications the attention they merit will gain knowledge and inspiration to do a job worthy of the best traditions of the foodservice industry.

PATRICK L. O'MALLEY
Chairman of the Board
Canteen Corporation;
President
National Restaurant Association

Preface

It was thirty years after graduation from a prestigious business school and the Class of '45 was holding its first reunion. In one corner of the hall a cluster of old grads got to talking about which member of the class had been most successful.

"You seem to have made out very well, Joe. How did your restaurant company do it?"

"The right product at the right time," said Joe. "Our biggest seller is a chicken dinner which costs us two dollars and we sell it for eight—and you can't beat six percent return on your investment."

There is certainly no doing without the dynamic business leader, the idea man, the crack salesman. But someone has to count the money, and account for it.

But who is to do it? And will the same person plan the use of money and decide where the earnings go? In a large enterprise with a special department for every function that question is not so imposing. But even owner-managers of small establishments may regard their time as better spent if they can "step over" the technical details of money management. And all of this may very well be. The question is, how wide does the boss step? How much of these details can be left to others so that he or she can concentrate on production and sales? Or, perhaps more to the point, how much does the manager need to know about these matters before they can safely be overstepped?

It's a matter of degree, we might say. It depends on the organization, the product and the market. No doubt. With few exceptions, however, as our authors explain, commercial foodservice profits and institutional foodservice budgets hang by delicate threads which require careful manipulation to avoid a collapsing stress at some point in the system.

So this is a book on foodservice accounting, for the manager and the prospective manager. It is not intended to make an accountant out of either. For some students it could turn out to be the introduction that led them into the accounting profession itself. For some operators it may end up being the book that allowed them *not to have to be* accountants. Which would be all right, too. Whatever happens, it will have served its purpose if it makes figures less intimidating and more informative to the average manager—and especially so if it allows the founder and principal stockholder to make 300 percent profit, even if he calls it six!

The book treats financial management mainly from the perspective of the independent operator. Some discussions imply an elaborate organizational structure. We trust the reader will on occasion accept this as a simplifying device for analyzing intricate management functions, many of which fall to one person in a small organization.

Professor Bolhuis, we believe, is eminently qualified to discuss these problems from a practical standpoint. He was a successful restaurateur in Detroit, was president of the Michigan Restaurant Association, and now teaches the subject as Chairman of Hotel-Restaurant Management, Asheville-Buncombe Technical Institute, in Asheville, North Carolina. His collaborator, Mr. Wolff, is a practicing Certified Public Accountant in Asheville, and lecturer in accounting at A-B Tech.

This textbook represents, in addition to the work of its principal authors, significant efforts on the part of NIFI staff members and their colleagues in foodservice management education. We are pleased to acknowledge, in particular, the contributions of:

William P. Fisher, Ph.D., executive vice president of the National Restaurant Association, and former member of the faculty of the School of Hotel Administration, Cornell University, who helped plan the book and prepared material for three chapters of the original manuscript.

Theodore J. Cooney, president of the National Institute for the Foodservice Industry, and retired vice president of Service Systems Corporation, who evaluated the manuscript in first draft, and

John Farr, vice president, corporate planning, of Canteen Corporation, and formerly instructor in hotel and restaurant accounting at Cornell University, who provided valuable critique and commentary on the manuscript in its initial and final phases.

As always, we are grateful to Chester G. Hall, Ph.D., executive vice president of the Institute, for his guidance and encouragement throughout the project.

NIFI, CHICAGO   FLOYD J. GREENE
15 March 1976   Editorial Director

Contents

PART ONE

ACCOUNTING FUNDAMENTALS, HISTORY AND PURPOSE

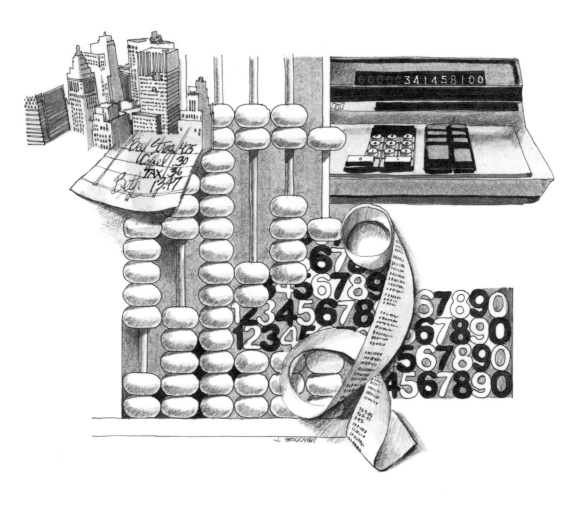

CHAPTER 1

BOOKKEEPING AND FINANCE

Stepping stones in the rise of industry

PURPOSE

To examine the close links between business enterprise and the financial arts, with a glance at some landmarks in their mutual progress over the past 200 years, and with special attention to the central theme of this text: Financial skill is an essential tool in the professional kit of today's successful foodservice·manager.

CONTENT

Why basic orientation in accounting principles and techniques is important to management

Some history of the growth of industry and of concurrent advances in accounting methods

The major branches of accounting

The users of accounting information

Bookkeeping vs. accounting: A conventional distinction

The Certified Public Accountant

"WHAT? BOOKKEEPING AND FINANCE? Why should I know about that? What I need to know, as a foodservice operator, is how to purchase food, prepare food and serve food. What the people want—that's what I need to know! I can hire a bookkeeper to take care of that other stuff for me."

Certainly this is not the speech of a professional foodservice manager. The professional knows he or she is part of the fastest-growing industry in the United States, an industry that ranks fourth in retail sales—over $70 billion annually—and employs more people than any other industry—approximately four million. As a professional the operator also knows that to do his job he must take every advantage of the tools and techniques available through modern management methods.

Perhaps the speaker is not really aware of the changes that have taken place in the foodservice industry in the past two hundred years. It is true that in the first century of its existence, the economy of the United States was based almost exclusively on agriculture. Foodservice operations in those times were relatively simple. Few demands were made on the businessman or farmer to keep accounting records. The restaurateur or tavern-keeper had little need to know anything more than rudimentary accounting, and management finance was as yet unheard of. It was near the end of the eighteenth century that the Industrial Revolution started the American people on a new way of life. Eli Whitney's invention of

the cotton gin in 1794 began the mechanization of agriculture, and his invention of a metal milling machine in 1798 forecast the day of machine tools and assembly-line production. The shift away from a predominantly agricultural economy was under way. With change in the air, new ideas and methods grew apace. Cyrus McCormick's invention of the reaper and related developments freed men from work on the farm and beckoned them to a life in the city. Before long, history would provide a further impetus—the War Between the States.

Along with other segments of society, the business community felt the shattering effects of the Civil War, which brought serious disruptions in commerce between the two sides and wrecked long-established financial relationships. The half-century following the war was marked by radical changes in the economy associated with Reconstruction and other major events of the time—land grants, the railroad boom and the winning of the West, along with the creation of a national banking system—all manifesting and contributing to further industrialization of the country. These events were naturally attended by other significant developments in the financial world, not the least of which was the growing use of the bank check as a substitute for cash in business transactions. A bank check is a written order drawn by a depositor ordering the bank to pay on demand a definite sum of money to the bearer. The check was not a wholly new instrument of exchange, but the economic revolution in the making may never have reached its present point without widespread reliance on this new-old method of settling debts.

Through the nineteenth and into the twentieth century scientific and technological advances continued. Men like William Kelly, who revolutionized steel-making; Goodyear, who discovered how to vulcanize rubber; Edison, in the field of electricity; and a parade of other engineering giants, made possible extraordinary developments in manufacturing and trade. These developments altered the form of ownership, hastened the growth of large corporations with absentee owners and hired managers, and inevitably heralded new concepts in finance and accounting. Huge amounts of fixed capital had to be procured, controlled and accounted for. The twentieth century was still young when history again shaped an event that greatly affected the lives of present and future generations—the First World War.

World War I made heavy demands on the industrial capacity of the United States. Advances in manufacturing and transportation accelerated by the war changed the economic picture and modified the living and eating habits of the people. The foodservice industry, using new refrigeration and processing methods, answered the demands of a population given more and more to eating away from home. Following the war, in the twenties and thirties, a number of restaurant chains came into being. Growth of the industry continued despite the Depression and slow economic recovery. The National Recovery Act forced a larger number of companies to keep comprehensive records. Social Security,

Workman's Compensation, and other social legislation not only brought more accounting into the picture, but compelled the foodservice industry to become more sophisticated in its operations and the operator to take a more professional approach to management.

World War II ushered in further change, both economic and social, and the foodservice industry found itself not only increasing in size but specializing as never before. Industrial catering, fast-food operations, ethnic restaurants and specialty houses, cafeterias and formal dining rooms, school lunch and other special catering now underwent rapid development. The federal government lowered its test for companies considered to be in interstate commerce. This and new state laws brought many additional business organizations under regulations requiring substantial record-keeping. Foodservice companies were no exception.

After World War II, manufacturers turned from defense to civilian production and found the market for hard goods largely saturated. However, among a people seeking respite from wartime pressures, new markets in the recreation sector of the economy were rapidly opening up. Investment capital was channeled more and more into "hospitality" industries gearing up to serve a more transient population with greater disposable income and with a much increased inclination to dine out. The foodservice industry was well on its way to becoming Big Business.

Today even a relatively small foodservice establishment needs substantial sums of money to finance its operations. Management, taxing authorities, owners and creditors require detailed records. With increased growth of the industry, more government control, growing union membership and higher financing costs, the manager must be a professional in more ways than one.

The modern foodservice manager recognizes the importance of the role played by the accountant in accumulating information for sound business decisions. And the knowledgeable operator recognizes that a basic knowledge of accounting and management finance is an essential tool in his or her own professional kit.

Accounting is basic to business. The maintenance of records required by government for tax purposes is essential. Reports discharging the company's obligations to owners, investors and suppliers are vital to good business practice. Of first importance in the present context are the services the accounting system provides to management as it records and summarizes all business transactions, and shapes these data into instruments for decision-making.

Accounting is so basic to business it has often been called the language of business. The manager who understands this language and is able to interpret the financial statements presented by the accountant is in a position to modify operations that are not successful and to improve on those that are. If management is to make intelligent decisions and operate the business efficiently it must have accurate reports and reliable estimates with which to work.

The professional foodservice operator may be a specialist in cafeteria, industrial feeding, formal dining room, luncheonette, or coffee shop operations.

Specialization in a particular area is common in other professions: law, medicine, education and, for that matter, accounting. The general practitioner may be competent in all areas to some degree, but often calls in the specialist when technical problems arise.

THE ACCOUNTING PROFESSION

Aside from general accounting, to some extent already described, the field of accounting may logically be divided into four areas of specialization: cost accounting, tax accounting, budgeting and governmental accounting.

Hotel and foodservice accounting is itself a specialized category in many respects. To handle the problems peculiar to our industry, some accounting firms are staffed by specialists in the hospitality industry as well as by consultants in taxation, cost and other areas of accounting. The names given to the various specialties fairly well describe the work done in those areas, but we will here elaborate briefly on the major categories.

Cost accounting. This specialized area of accounting examines the cost of doing business. In the foodservice industry, a cost accountant might estimate the cost of serving a meal or a particular menu item. Specifically, the accountant might compute the cost of preparing a baked potato, a particular cut of steak, a vegetable or salad, and may also compute the cost of labor involved in serving the item. The cost accountant projects the cost of an item and, after the item has been served, determines its actual cost. Projected and actual costs are then compared in evaluating the operations of the business.

Tax accounting. Tax regulations are constantly changing. Having struggled with individual income tax returns, we are all aware of some of the complexities of this form of accounting. Taxes levied on a business, whether it be a proprietorship, partnership or corporation, can become very involved. Experts who spend their lives keeping abreast of these laws are often our only recourse in solving some of the problems arising out of business activities. Taxes can have a direct effect on some business decisions. In choosing between buying equipment or leasing it, for example, the tax consequences may be the deciding factor.

Budgeting. This branch of accounting concerns itself with business planning. Many accountants make a specialty of developing operational data which will enable management to project sales and costs with reasonable accuracy. These data draw heavily on accounting records, so the budget becomes a vehicle also for evaluating past performance. It further serves as a control device as the accountant compares projected figures with actual results of operations. In working with historical and anticipated events, the foodservice budgeter may present his calculations in terms of total sales or in terms of specific menu items. In either case it is important to use the budget as a dynamic system for checking and adjusting sales and costs throughout the operating period.

Governmental accounting. This is a special system of accounting attuned to the requirements of government. Many of the record-keeping and accounting mechanisms are the same as those used in the commercial world. But there is a fundamental difference in approach, occasioned by the fact that government is constituted to provide service, not to make a profit. Private educational and nonprofit institutions use similar systems.

ACCOUNTING IN FOODSERVICE AND LODGING

The hotel industry early developed accounting methods to suit its special needs. Since food and beverage service represent a large and distinct part of hotel operations, it soon became evident that this aspect of the business required its own accounting procedures. It was a natural development for some accountants working in the hotel industry to evolve as specialists in foodservice accounting. Independently the great restaurant institutions of Europe and America, from the sixteenth century on, contributed to this result. These accountants are referred to as *hospitality industry* specialists, in keeping with the umbrella term now generally applied to hotels, restaurants, resorts, clubs and similar "guestronomic" enterprises.

As we have noted, large-scale foodservice organizations have proliferated in recent decades, and not only in Western society. Fast-food operations in particular have been exported to once remote parts of the world. And this expansion has in a significant degree been made possible by sound, universally accepted accounting practices.

The benefits of good record-keeping and financial analysis are of first interest to managers and owners, but others outside the immediate business family are legitimately concerned. Among these are its investors, its creditors and, not the least, taxing and regulatory agencies of government. The greatest demands on the accounting system are those made by the federal government in the collection of income taxes from corporations and individuals. This is a voluntary system of taxation in the sense that the taxpayer initiates the process by declaring his or her income and computing the tax payment due the government. The penalty that may be assessed for late, improper or fraudulent tax returns places a serious burden of responsibility on the business manager. This means careful verification of the accuracy and completeness of operating records, which requires close cooperation with the accounting department. The government also requires numerous reports to its bureaus and branches, many of which call for technical skill in preparation and often demand the services of a trained accountant.

In many companies the owners do not actively participate in management. They, or a board of directors representing investors, will select a management team and guide general policy. Actual day-to-day operations are left to the managers they have selected. The owners would be unable to exercise close control, being physically removed from the scene of operations. In view of their investment in the company, they are nevertheless interested in its financial success. Evaluating the data furnished by the accountant, the owners can judge how well the restaurant is being operated and thereby determine the effectiveness of its management. Prospective investors can also make good use of the company's financial statements as sources of information on its profitability.

A good credit rating is important to a restaurant, as it is to any business operation. Since some foodservice operations buy many items on credit, it is essential that they be able to present prospective creditors with evidence of their ability to pay. Financial statements usually provide the necessary information. Whether the restaurant requires long-term credit, as for the purchase of a building and equipment, weekly or monthly credit for food purchases, or a line of credit at the bank for working capital, these statements can tell a lot about a company's financial strength and reliability.

The function of accounting is to record, classify and summarize business transactions in monetary terms. Although this function embraces the work of both the accountant and the bookkeeper, a technical difference is recognized in the accounting profession, and in the business world generally, and will be observed throughout this text. According to this convention, *bookkeeping* is concerned essentially with recording and summarizing financial transactions. *Accounting* is concerned with further summarization of data and interpretation of it to serve the purposes of management. It is an oversimplification to define accounting as advanced bookkeeping, but in this country that suggests a distinction based on the formal education of the individual so engaged. While the bookkeeper may not always be as much involved in the ultimate use of the data he or she compiles, the professional accountant is specially trained in evaluating and projecting the operations of a business enterprise through the use of financial information.

The role of the accountant in the business organization has not always been fully appreciated. Yesterday's accountant may have been looked upon as a keeper of records who only gathered the results of the past. Little emphasis was placed on the kind of advice the accountant could give, and too often that advice may have been imperfectly understood and used. In the dynamic business world of today, the accountant is assuming an important role in the management process. The accountant now accumulates the data and organizes it in a meaningful presentation enabling the manager, owner, creditor, governmental agency or investor to understand the information and evaluate the condition and capabilities of the company. The modern accountant is not only expected to make suggestions for corrective action, but to take a position in management decisions and to help in formulating company policy.

Some accountants, having successfully completed a comprehensive test given by the American Institute of Certified Public Accountants, and after serving a period of apprenticeship under a Certified Public Accountant, receive the designation of C.P.A. The C.P.A. is a recognized expert in accounting and taxation. He usually has a general knowledge of all areas of accounting—general, cost, tax, budget, and governmental—and may specialize in serving certain industries. Some accountants and accounting firms specialize in foodservice management finance, as previously noted. Stockholders, creditors, bankers and others with financial interest in a company may require the company to have a Certified Public Accountant ex-amine its accounting records and give a professional opinion on the reliability of its financial statements.

SUMMARY

The foodservice industry over the past two hundred years has developed into big business. The foodservice operator must recognize he or she is a professional, and often a specialist, in an industry with more than $70 billion annually in gross sales, and employing approximately four million persons. As a professional the foodservice manager must be educated in many areas, including bookkeeping, accounting and management finance.

Because of the size and complexity of modern hotel and restaurant enterprises, accountants · with special qualifications in the hospitality industry have emerged in recent decades. Often these accountants belong to firms who specialize as management consultants to the industry. These companies are often staffed by Certified Public Accountants who are recognized experts in this field of accounting and are qualified to give expert opinion as to the reliability of financial statements.

The professional foodservice manager recognizes that the accounting process is designed to serve interests other than those of management. The financial statements produced for the company are also of legitimate interest to taxing authorities, owners and creditors.

The manager need not be an accountant himself, but should know enough about the principles and practices of accounting to appreciate the important contributions the accountant can make to good business decisions.

Accounting is so basic to business it has often been called the language of business. The manager who understands this language and is able to interpret the financial statements presented by the accountant is in a position to modify operations that are not successful and to improve on those that are.

STUDY QUESTIONS

1. Discuss briefly the interdependence of industry and finance as witnessed by their mutual growth since the beginning of the Industrial Revolution some 200 years ago.

2. Defend the authors' general thesis that the foodservice manager needs to know accounting principles to compete in today's fast-growing industry.

3. Name the four major areas of specialization in the accounting profession.

4. In what essential way does the accounting system used by government differ from that used in private industry?

5. Name and describe two ways in which a company's financial reports are used by other than its own management.

6. Explain in a few words the increasing reliance on financial reports as a foodservice company expands its operations.

7. Define accounting, and explain the technical difference between the functions of the bookkeeper and the accountant as generally recognized in the U.S. business community.

8. Describe in about 200 words the role of the professional accountant as a technician, planner and general consultant in financial management.

CHAPTER 2

THE ACCOUNTING FUNCTION

A quick review of things we never knew

PURPOSE

To explore the underlying principles and some of the basic techniques of bookkeeping and accounting which the manager needs to know in interpreting financial statements; and to recognize the importance of these statements in the decision-making process.

CONTENT

The Basic Nature of Accounting

Cash, or Single-Entry, Bookkeeping

The Double-Entry System of Accounting

The Flow of Accounting Data

Debit and Credit—The T Account

The Accounting Equation: Assets = Liabilities + Capital

ACCOUNTING IS BASIC TO BUSINESS. All of us become involved in it to some extent in our ordinary experience. We sell our services and receive income; rent an apartment; buy a house with a mortgage loan; finance the purchase of a car; incur expenses for utilities; pay cash for food and other goods and services. As individuals and as a family we are, in a sense, in business. Although most of us do not think of our personal lives in this way, some people do formalize their financial affairs, as an accountant would do, with a book for income and a book for expenses (journals, in the business world) and live on a budget. The only accounting device many of us ever use is our checkbook, but when it comes time for income tax returns we may find that additional records would be useful.

To understand how accounting works it helps to bring it close to home, but we shouldn't overwork the analogy. In one very important respect our private finances are unlike business finances: we are not primarily engaged in exchanging money, goods and services for profit.

ACCOUNTING SYSTEMS

Profit-making enterprises usually need fairly elaborate accounting procedures, but many small businesses do very little more accounting than the average householder. The simple method they use is called *cash* or *single-entry* accounting, which may actually involve keeping only two books of record—one for sales and the other for expenses. In totaling these figures and comparing them the bookkeeper would show an excess of income as a profit, and an excess of expenses as a loss.

But this form of accounting would be unworkable for a larger business, which might need, among other things, to make adjustments in inventory, amortize insurance and other prepaid expenses, and accrue certain expenses (record them as they occur and defer payment)—accounting procedures that would be almost impossible with a single-entry system.

Although a business must keep records, its outlay for accounting should correspond to the size and needs of its operations. It should not cost more to operate the accounting system than that system returns in information of value to the business. In other words, each department should—in its way—show a profit.

As noted in Chapter 1, accounting data should be gathered and presented in a manner that satisfies all individuals and organizations that have a valid interest in receiving it. The *double-entry* system of accounting has long been accepted by the business community as the most effective means of accomplishing these purposes. There is indeed nothing new in double-entry bookkeeping. History gives ample evidence of its use as far back as the fourteenth century, and to this day it continues to serve commercial establishments of every kind, size and complexity. Each industry has developed, within the double-entry frame-

SOME BASIC DEFINITIONS

In common with the individual, a business *owns* things and it *owes* for things.

It *owns* cash, merchandise, buildings and equipment. It may also own less tangible things like the patent to a manufacturing process, the right-of-way across another's land, the copyright on a book.

A business *owes* for goods and services it acquires on promise to pay: money it borrows, articles bought on credit, leased facilities, labor before wages, utilities, transportation.

It is helpful to relate the language of business to ordinary terminology, but we should observe caution in doing so. Accounting is a special language that often assigns a special meaning to an ordinary word.

Things of value which a company owns are called *assets*. What it owes are *liabilities,* which represent the creditors' share of the assets. The owners' share of the assets is classified as *capital*. These are basic terms the accountant uses in summarizing data on financial statements.

A mainstay in accounting concepts is represented by the term *equity*. The idea of equity is perhaps not as free-standing as the three basic elements named above, but supports a fundamental view of them all—from the standpoint of rights to property. An equity can generally be defined as a right. Usually a company owns more than it owes, and the remainder represents *its* equity in the assets, or the value of the owners' share in the business. This latter description applies to capital, which is otherwise known as owners' equity. Similarly, liabilities can be described as creditors' equity.

Using these terms in logical sequence, we may state the accounting equation: Assets = Equity = Liabilities + Capital. It is, however, conventionally written Assets = Liability + Capital ($A = L + C$).

The term asset derives from a word meaning assigned. In the legal sense assets are resources that are assignable in the settlement of debts. A liability, generally speaking, is a debt.

Capital, in the lexicon of economics, means wealth. As applied to business enterprise it is commonly understood to mean wealth that is put to work to generate more wealth. In the strict accounting sense the term capital signifies that amount of property owned at a specified time, as distinct from income during a given period. Capital represents net worth, that part of the assets which is free and clear of charges and claims.

To review the three fundamental terms from the viewpoint of equity (rights to property): If we identify *assets* as values that can be traded, then those values to which creditors have the right are reckoned as *liabilities,* and those values to which the owners have the right are reckoned as *capital*.

Financial Statement Users

Management		Government		Creditors		Owners or Investors

⬆

Financial Statement

Financial Statements
Balance Sheet
Income Statement
Change in Financial Position
Capital Statement

⬆

Ledger

General Ledger

⬆

JOURNALS

Cash Receipts Journal		Cash Payments Journal		Purchase Journal		Sales Journal		General Journal

⬆

Source Data

Cash Received		Guest Check		Time Cards		Checks Issued by Company		Invoices Received by Company		Contract for purchase of equipment

EXHIBIT 2–1 The flow of accounting information, from original source to ultimate user.

work, a method appropriate to its particular requirements. The "Uniform System of Accounts for Restaurants," for example, is widely used in the food-service industry. This publication will be described in a later chapter.

Our emphasis in this text is on the *application* of accounting information by management as it evaluates, plans and controls. Future events are built on the record, but the primary function of *accounting* is nevertheless to *account—* for business events that have already occurred. How it performs this essential task is our main concern in the present chapter.

Initially the accounting process identifies and records each transaction as it occurs. Then it classifies and accumulates these data, and ultimately summarizes them in financial statements that (1) show the financial position of the firm at a *point* in time; and (2) describe operations during a selected *period* of time.

The bookkeeper and accountant maintain a constant flow of information as they record and report the operations of a business enterprise. (See Exhibit 2–1 herewith and Exhibit 4–1 in Chapter 4.) In brief, the pattern of flow is:

Voucher → Journal → Ledger → Financial
Statements

The voucher (original source material) for a given transaction may take the form of a checkbook, bank statement, food check, cash register tape, time card or minute book of a corporation. The transaction represented by the voucher is identified and then entered, in the order of its occurrence, in the *journal* designated for that class of trans-

action. The journal is referred to as a *book of original entry,* since it is the first place in which a transaction is recorded in the accounting process. The journals kept by an organization thus provide a running record of all transactions in chronological order (see Exhibit 2–2, p. 16).

The next evolution in the flow of data, from the *journal* to the *ledger,* is called "posting." Entries are grouped in individual accounts corresponding to the classification of data carried in the journals. The ledger account does not record all transactions, but shows totals for transactions of a particular kind. Both these books of record are therefore necessary to get us to this point in the accounting process. Thereafter, ledger entries are summarized in the financial statements. Each of these, the balance sheet, the income statement, the statement of changes in financial position (cash statement), and others, has a function of its own to be discussed further in a later chapter. Exhibits 2–3 and 2–4 are presented on pp. 18–19 as examples.

In a small foodservice operation with relatively few daily transactions, one journal might be sufficient. When only one is used, entries to the journal should contain information indicating the nature of the transaction. In the classical system five basic journals are used: cash receipts, cash payments, purchases, sales, and general. Not less important but in a somewhat special category is the payroll.

The *cash receipts journal* records all transmittals of money to the company, including cash payment of guest checks (often also recorded in the sales journal), money borrowed from the bank, money

Sample Journal Entries
ABC Restaurant

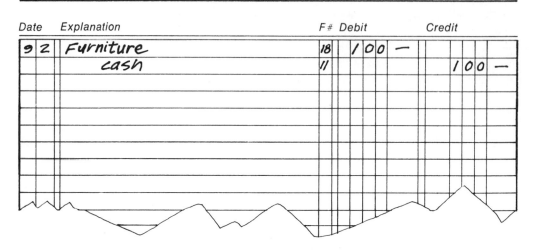

Date		Explanation	F #	Debit						Credit				
9	2	Furniture	18	1	0	0	—							
		cash	11							1	0	0	—	

Sample Ledger Entries
ABC Restaurant

FURNITURE   F # 18

		DEBIT								CREDIT					
Date		Explanation	page	Amount				Date		Explanation	page	Amount			
9	2	Purc. FURN.	√ 1	1	0	0	—								

CASH   F # 11

						Date		Explanation	page	Amount			
						9	2	FURN.	√ 1	1	0	0	—

Standard printed sheets are blank, titles and labels to be entered by bookkeeper.
Extra labeling shown here for instructional purposes.

EXHIBIT 2–2   Example of journal entries and their posting in corresponding ledger accounts.

from investors, repayment of employee loans, and cash received from any other source.

The *cash payments journal* records all cash disbursements, noting the amount to whom the money was paid and the date. The voucher, invoice, or check number will further identify the reason for the expenditure, which may be payment of wages, purchases from vendors, mortgage payments, payment of taxes withheld—any transaction involving the transfer of money from the company. Since most payments are made by check, this journal is essentially a record of checks written by the company showing the purpose for which they were issued.

The *purchase journal* records all purchases made on credit, such as purchases of food, small items of equipment, advertising, utilities and other services. Entries show the source of the item, the amount purchased, the vendor, and purchase classification.

The *sales journal* might more appropriately be called the sales-on-account journal, but for the sake of brevity is known as the sales journal. It records only credit sales, in which the buyer does not pay cash. The most likely transactions handled this way in a foodservice would probably be catering service and accommodations for banquets, meetings, conventions, and the like.

The *general journal* records miscellaneous transactions which do not fit in any of the other journals.

Since information in the journal is now to be posted to the appropriate ledger account, sufficient identification is necessary to ensure proper posting. This should include the account title and number, the date, the side of the account on which it will be entered, and the journal page from which the posting is being transferred. If classified as a *debit* it will be posted on the *left* side; if a *credit*, it will be posted on the *right* side.

Whoa, now! What's with this left side, right side, debit and credit?

You're right. Two new words have just been introduced into the picture. We have, up to this point, been trying to show the foodservice manager that the accounting system can be used as an information system; also that financial statements provided by the accountant can be used in the decision-making process without a technical knowledge of bookkeeping. It is vital, however, for the manager to know the source of the data accumulated, where the data is recorded, and how it is summarized. With an understanding of these procedures, one can see meaningful relationships between figures representing certain operations, and follow their development. This makes it possible to reckon with more than the bottom line on the income and expense statement (profit or loss), and with more than increases and decreases in the proprietorship figures on the balance sheet.

BOOKKEEPING TECHNIQUE

Although the debit and credit sides of an account are absolutely essential to double-entry accounting, and their use is as commonplace to the accountant as ham and eggs are to the restaurateur, the terms themselves are not so easy to justify. As applied in accounting technique the words debit and credit may

ABC Foodservice Co., Inc.

BALANCE SHEET

Dec. 31, 19xx

ASSETS

Current Assets . . . .

  Cash . . . .

  Inventories—food supplies . . . .

  Total Prepaid Expenses . . . .

    Total Current Assets . . . .

Fixed Assets

	Cost	Less: Accumulated Depreciation	
Building & Land	. . . .	. . . .	
Furnishings & Equipment	. . . .	. . . .	
Sign	. . . .	. . . .	
Automobiles	. . . .	. . . .	
Total Fixed Assets	. . . .	. . . .	. . . .

Total Assets . . . .

LIABILITIES AND CAPITAL

Current Liabilities

  Accounts Payable . . . .

  Accrued Expenses . . . .

    Total Current Liabilities . . . .

Capital Stock and Retained Earnings

  Capital Stock . . . .

  Retained Earnings . . . .

    Total Capital . . . .

Total Liabilities and Capital . . . .

EXHIBIT 2–3 A typical balance sheet.

ABC Foodservice Co., Inc.

INCOME & EXPENSE STATEMENT

Jan. 1, 19xx to Dec. 31, 19xx

FOOD SALES

Cost of Food Sold . . . .

Inventory Jan. 1, 19xx . . . .
Purchases for period . . . .

   Total . . . .

Less: Inventory, Dec. 31, 19xx . . . .

Net Cost of Food Sold . . . .

Gross Profit . . . .

Cost of Payroll

Salaries and wages . . . .
Employee meals . . . .
Payroll taxes . . . .

   Total payroll cost . . . .

Operating Expenses

Repairs and maintenance . . . .
Utilities . . . .
Linen expense . . . .
Office expense and accounting . . . .
Depreciation . . . .
Taxes . . . .
Insurance . . . .

   Total operating expense . . . .

   Total payroll and operating expense . . . .

Operating Profit or Loss . . . .

   Other Income . . . .

NET PROFIT OR LOSS . . . .

EXHIBIT 2–4　A typical income & expense statement.

seem so far removed from their dictionary meaning as to defy logical explanation. Some authors, in fact, regard them as impossible stumbling blocks and advise the reader to forget logic and accept the convention: debits means left, credit means right. For many of us that is probably good advice. If, however, your passion for wherefores is overwhelming, stay with the following discussion.

Looking at Exhibit 2–2 you will see examples of a ledger sheet and a journal sheet. You will note that the two halves of the ledger sheet are identical except for the column headings, Debit and Credit, and that the journal sheet has separate columns to the right, similarly labeled. Entries are made on the right or left side of the ledger, or in the right- or left-hand column of the journal, depending on whether they are debits or credits. *Debit* is a word accountants use for entries on the left, and *credit* a word for entries on the right (rather arbitrarily, some would say). These terms also tell the accountant various other things, but in the respect that debit is left and credit is right, they do not vary.

All accounting transactions affect one of five classes of accounts: assets, expense, liabilities, capital (proprietorship) or revenues (sales). An entry on the credit or debit side of the record—ledger or journal—always affect these accounts the same way. (It should therefore be evident that if we are to receive good information, the bookkeeping department had better know right from left!) An entry on the left-debit side indicates an increase in assets and expense accounts. (Why? Ask not yet.) An entry on this same *left-debit* side indicates a

decrease in liability, capital and revenue (sales) accounts. (Before re-reading the last two statements, which you will need to do at least once, review your basic definitions for assets, liabilities, etc.) On the other hand, an entry on the *right-credit* side indicates a *decrease* in assets and expense, and an *increase* in liability, capital and revenue (sales) accounts.

Double-entry accounting is so called because there must be two entries made for each transaction. For example (Exhibit 2–2), the ABC Restaurant purchased furniture, and this financial transaction was duly noted in the journal. Since the transaction increased the furniture account, it is shown as a debit (plus) to that account; however, cash was used to pay for the furniture, which reduced the cash account, and this is shown by a credit (minus) entry in the cash account. The transaction was first shown in the journal, as the book of original entry, and then posted to the individual ledger accounts for furniture and cash. These two accounts thus show a credit balance in cash of $100, and a debit balance in furniture of $100, and the ledger is in balance.

A fundamental thing to be said about these rigorous debit-credit, left-right, plus-minus rules in accounting technique is that they permit equilibrium to be maintained between the two sides of the basic accounting equation (about which more later).

The greatest merit in double-entry, no doubt, is that it allows ready assembly of summary information for business decisions. The marvel is how it manages to do this so effectively for all interested parties. Much of the "marvel" is certainly to be ascribed to the rigor in the system. But in that one seems to see also the rigid hand of custom at work. How else explain, for example, debiting an asset? You may get some flak from the traditionalist, but if you are a word purist and keep seeing a common root in the terms debit and debt (as well you might), consider this:

Counting money is one thing. *Accounting* for it takes us a step further, and double-entry must always go that far. This means we have at least two perspectives on every business event. Take the cash account, for instance. We receive money and that's an asset, a plus. Do we "plus" an asset on the debit side of the account to remind us that for every "get" there has to be a "give"— and that we must also "plus" it on the credit side? That may be a fair rationalization.

Ledger accounts are sometimes referred to as "T" accounts because of the conventional shape they take, with a vertical line dividing the debits and credits and with a crosspiece for the title of the account, as illustrated here:

Furniture and Fixtures
$100

The whole structure of double-entry accounting can be similarly represented, with a giant T showing the basic relationship between assets on one side and liabilities and capital on the other. When this is done it can be seen that we have T's within T's and the pattern becomes wondrously complex. Such a diagram as that presented in Exhibit 2–5 may not be the best place to begin learning the system, but the student will find it a useful reference in keeping his debits and credits and pluses and minuses on their own side of the road (see p. 22).

With respect to the matter of how double-entry keeps accounts in balance, a generalization or two may be in order. Whenever we add a value to one side of the big T we must add an equal value to the other side; likewise, when we subtract from one side we must subtract equally from the other. The alternative is to change *two* accounts on the *same* side of the big T, adding to one and subtracting from the other in equal amounts. The net result will be zero change on that side, and the general balance is undisturbed.

As noted in our diagram of the flow of accounting data, the totals in the various journals are compiled periodically and posted to the ledger accounts. In the foodservice industry, ledger accounts are usually set up in accordance with common practices recommended by the National Restaurant Association. A uniform system makes it easier to compare the operations of one establishment with those of another. The financial statements on which these comparisons are based also provide a source of valuable industry-wide statistics. As our discussions proceed, the student will be concerned more and more with the information contained in these summary statements (see Exhibits 2–3 and 2–4). It will become clear how the *income statement* tells management the results of operations over a period of time, and how the *balance sheet* tells where the company stands at a given instant. The element tying these two statements to-

ASSETS = LIABILITIES + CAPITAL

Cash

+ Dr.	− Cr.
$10,000	$200
$5,000	$1,500

Accts. Receivable

+ Dr.	− Cr.
$500	

Inventory

+ Dr.	− Cr.
$1,500	

Equipment

+ Dr.	− Cr.
$600	

Notes Payable

− Dr.	+ Cr.
	5,000

Accts. Payable

− Dr.	+ Cr.
	$600

Owner's Equity

− Dr.	+ Cr.
	$10,000

Revenues

− Dr.	+ Cr.
	$500

Expenses

+ Dr.	− Cr.
$200	

EXHIBIT 2-5

A general view of how individual T-accounts fit into the Big T of accounting. This chart is mainly for reference, showing how the accounting equation is kept in balance and where the pluses and minuses go. But you will note that the dollar entries agree with the analysis of transactions on succeeding pages, and that debit and credit totals across the board equalize.

gether is the profit (or loss) figure on the income statement, a figure reflected on the balance sheet as a change in owners' equity (capital).

THE ACCOUNTING EQUATION

When the ledger accounts are summarized, we will recall, the total of the debits must equal the total of the credits. In other words the total amount owned by the foodservice company must equal the total amount owed. (The latter includes owners' investment—the capital account—which represents an obligation of the company.) This required equilibrium in the accounting structure, conforming to the big-T analysis referred to above (and shown in Exhibit 2–5), is also expressed in algebraic terms, giving us the fundamental accounting equation:

$$A = L + C$$

Assets equal Liabilities plus Capital. If all values owned by the company are added up, the total must equal the amount the company owes, plus its own

equity in the business. Stated another way, liabilities represent the creditors' share, and capital represents the owners' share, of the assets.

Now let's see what effect some typical transactions will have on this accounting equation.

Event I. Two businessmen establish a restaurant company by going to the bank and depositing $10,000. The equation stands:

$$A = L + C$$
$$\text{Cash} = L + \text{Capital}$$
$$\$10,000 = 0 + \$10,000$$

Explanation: The restaurant company has cash Assets of $10,000. Liabilities are zero. The amount of Capital is $10,000. All assets are in the form of owners' equity because the partners deposited their own money. (There being no liabilities, the owners have all rights to the assets of the company.)

Event II. Seeing a need for more money, the owners go back to the bank and borrow $5,000 in the name of the company. Effect on the equation:

	$A =$	$L + C$
Prior balance	$10,000 =	0 + $10,000
This transaction	5,000 =	$5,000 + 0
New balance	$15,000 =	$5,000 + $10,000

Explanation: Assets increased by $5,000 in new cash. Liabilities now show $5,000 (note payable). Capital is unchanged. The company has $5,000 more in assets but this is represented by a change in creditors' rights only ($5,000 owed to the bank). Owners' share in the assets (capital) remains at $10,000.

Event III. The owners now decide to buy a piece of equipment. Their supplier is willing to extend the company credit for the purchase, so the partners elect to buy the equipment on account and conserve cash. The value (cost) of the new unit is $600. This transaction affects our equation as follows:

$$
\begin{array}{rcl}
 & A = & L + C \\
\text{Prior balance} \ \$15,000 = & \$5,000 + \$10,000 \\
\text{This transaction} \ \ \ \ 600 = & 600 + 0 \\
\hline
\text{New balance} \ \$15,600 = & \$5,600 + \$10,000
\end{array}
$$

Explanation: Assets increase again, by $600. Liabilities increase by an equal amount (account payable). Capital is unchanged. The company now has assets in the form of cash and equipment. It also has liabilities of two kinds, under notes payable and accounts payable. The latter represents a further change in creditors' rights ($600 owed to the equipment sup-

plier). Owners' rights still stand at $10,000, the original capital investment.

Event IV. The owners next pay rent of $200. This is the amount due for part of a month during the period the building and facilities are being readied for business, a disbursement affecting the equation in this way:

$$
\begin{array}{rcl}
 & A = & L + C \\
\text{Prior balance} \ \$15,600 = & \$5,600 + \$10,000 \\
\text{This transaction} \ \ -200 = & -200 \\
\hline
\text{New balance} \ \$15,400 = & \$5,600 + \$ \ 9,800
\end{array}
$$

Explanation: Assets reduced $200 by a decrease in cash. Liabilities unchanged. Capital reduced $200 by an expense of that amount. A new element, expense, has now entered the equation, shown as a charge against capital (owner's equity) on the right side of the equation, and as a charge against assets on the left side of the equation. We will

see this better if we add a new line expanding the dimensions of C (capital) to include investment and expenses; expanding L (liabilities) to include notes payable and accounts payable; and expanding A (assets) to include cash and equipment. The effect of Event IV is thus seen to be:

	A	=	L	+	C
	(Cash + Equip.)	=	$\left(\begin{smallmatrix}\text{Notes} \\ \text{Pay.}\end{smallmatrix} + \begin{smallmatrix}\text{Accts.} \\ \text{Pay.}\end{smallmatrix}\right)$ +		(Investment − Expenses)
Prior balance	($15,000 + $600)	=	($5,000 + $600)	+	$10,000
This transaction	−200	=			−200
New balance	($14,800 + $600)	=	($5,000 + $600)	+	$ 9,800

Event V. The owners decide it is time to build up some inventory, and order merchandise valued at $1,500. Terms

of the purchase call for cash. In abbreviated form the equation shows this effect:

$$
\begin{array}{lrcl}
& A & = & L \quad + \quad C \\
\text{Prior balance} & \$15,400 & = & \$5,600 \quad + \quad \$9,800 \\
\text{This transaction} & 1,500 & & \\
& -1,500 & = & 0 \\
\hline
\text{New balance} & \$15,400 & = & \$15,400
\end{array}
$$

Explanation: This demonstrates the other way of maintaining equilibrium in the accounting record: Two equal and opposite changes are made on the assets side, liabilities and capital are not changed, and the equation remains in balance.

If, as before, we expand the assets side, including this time an account for inventory, we would have:

	A		$=$	L	$+$	C
	(Cash + Equip. + Inv.)		=	(Notes + Accts. Pay)	+	$\left(\begin{array}{c}\text{Invest.}\\ -\text{ Exp.}\end{array}\right)$
Previous balance	$14,800 + $600		=	$5,000 + $600	+	$9,800
This transaction	−1,500	+ 1,500	=			0
New balance	$13,300 + $600	+ 1,500	=	$5,000 + $600	+	$9,800

In this transaction the company is giving up some of the asset *cash,* but in exchange is receiving an equal amount of the asset *inventory.* Since it is only changing the form of these assets from cash to inventory, no expense has taken place and the liability side of the equation does not change. Capital is also unchanged and equality between the two sides is undisturbed.

Event VI. The restaurant now opens its doors and sells $500 worth of food to banquet customers. Let's go immediately to our expanded equation to see the effect of this transaction:

	A			$=$	L	$+$	C
	(Cash + Accts. Rec. + Equip. + Inv.)			=	(Notes + Accts. Pay.)	+	$\left(\begin{array}{cc}\text{Invest.} & -\text{ Exp.}\\ & +\text{ Rev.}\end{array}\right)$
Pr. bal.	$13,300 + $600	+ $1,500	=	$5,000 + $600	+	$9,800
This Trans.	500		=				+ $500
New bal.	$13,800 + $600	+ $1,500	=	$5,000 + $600	+	$9,800	+ $500

Explanation: Both sides change equally. Assets increase $500 under a new account, accounts receivable. Capital increases $500 under a new account, revenues. Liabilities are unchanged. Cash is not affected since the banquet sale was made on credit, but the net result is the same: A change in assets (A) is balanced by a change in capital (C), and our inviolable accounting equation remains an equation.[1]

Without seeking to qualify as an operating bookkeeper or accountant, the student can see from the foregoing examples how the various "T" accounts in the ledger fit into the structure of the big "T" which balances assets (A) against liabilities (L) and capital (C), and how they keep the book always ready to supply data for a position statement at any time, and for an income & expense statement summarizing operations for any given period.

SUMMARY

The accounting function is not only basic to business but is familiar to us in our daily lives. Individuals and family units form a kind of business unit, although we may not recognize it as such. Our personal accounting is usually very simple, but some people may make it more systematic by using books of record for expense and income and a budget for regulating their spending. In the small business the accounting function is often not much more detailed than this. This form of accounting is often

---

1. For simplification we treat this transaction only as it affects assets (cash) and capital (revenue) positively. As explained later (see Chap. 7), also involved are a negative change in assets (inventory) and capital (expense) when cost factors are considered.

referred to as the *cash* or *single-entry* system of accounting.

History indicates that some form of accounting has always been used by civilized man. As civilization advanced, as the world's population and commerce grew, more sophisticated forms of accounting were needed. *Double-entry* bookkeeping, the system developed to meet this need, has served business enterprises for hundreds of years despite their ever-increasing complexity.

Accounting information flows from original source material to the journals, where it is accumulated and classified. Next the amounts are posted to the individual accounts in the ledger. From the ledger, where the amounts are totaled, the figures are summarized in the financial statements. The foodservice operator makes continuous use of the financial statements in the decision-making process. The *balance sheet* shows the position of the company at a point in time, while the *income & expense* statement tells the activities of the company over a period of time.

Debit and credit are terms used by the accountant to indicate the side—left or right—of the ledger or the appropriate column of the journal on which an entry is to be made. Debit entries (left side) indicate an increase in assets and expense accounts, and indicate a decrease in liability, revenue (sales) and capital accounts. Credit entries (right side) indicate the opposite in each case.

The accounting equation, $A = L + C$ (Assets = Liabilities + Capital), tells us that things owned by the company must equal the things owed to creditors and investors.

STUDY QUESTIONS

1. Describe briefly the flow of accounting information, naming the principal documents in the system.
2. In the practical sense, what do *debit* and *credit* mean to an accountant?
3. Define the term *assets,* and describe assets from the viewpoint of the business operator.
4. Define the term *equity,* and describe equity from the viewpoint of the company's investors and creditors.
5. How do entries on the debit side of an account affect expense, capital, liability, income, assets?
6. What is the fundamental accounting equation? Describe the general procedure whereby this equation is kept in balance.
7. Construct a mental model of the double-entry system which allows you to see how it facilitates record-keeping and the summarizing of accounting data.
8. What general distinction do you draw between the *bookkeeping* function and the *accounting* function as these terms are conventionally used?
9. What is the main purpose of the balance sheet?
10. What does the income & expense statement mainly tell us about a business?

CHAPTER 3

TRADITIONS GUIDING THE ACCOUNTANT

Rules he lives by—and some he lives with

PURPOSE

To review some of the fundamental concepts that have developed in the accounting profession through the years, standardizing the operating procedures observed by bookkeepers and accountants, and laying a universal ground for analyzing the financial activities of business enterprises and establishing their worth.

CONTENT

The How and Why of Accounting Precepts

Some Governing Principles Described

    The "business entity"

    The "going concern"

    Periodicity of accounts

    Matching expense to income

    Consistency in accounting procedure

    Full disclosure

    Money as the criterion of value

    Objectivity in accounting

    The accountant's conservatism

    Materiality of error

    Income recognition

    Expense recognition

THE ACCOUNTANT IS WELL AWARE that his product, the financial statement, will be used by many people and organizations for different reasons. Managers need the information to make business decisions. They may require not only an income & expense statement and a balance sheet, but various supplemental reports analyzing a particular item in detail or summarizing operations from a certain perspective. Investors are interested in the security of their money and in earnings on their investment. Creditors need to be assured that they will be paid for goods and services rendered. The government is not interested exclusively for tax purposes. Regulatory and statistics-gathering agencies at various levels of government have special reasons for being interested in the accountant's product.

Accountants recognize that in serving these diverse interests they must use a language common to all. The food-service operator deals with local suppliers, with companies operating across the country, and even with business enterprises in other parts of the world. The accounting system used must be based on principles that all accountants follow and that management anywhere will understand.

The development of a universally accepted accounting system has not been a simple phenomenon. To understand how it evolved may be as difficult as it is sometimes to realize that the giant Ford Motor Company started in a small, barn-like building on Bagley Avenue in Detroit.

The principles governing the accounting function have developed over the years with the growth of business activity and the need to regulate it. These principles are not laws, in the legal sense, or in the sense of scientific and mathematical laws. They are more in the nature of ideas—concepts and conventions—about what is logical and right in business transactions. Because of the importance of agreed-to principle and practice, leaders of the accounting profession gather periodically to consider and modify these rules in accordance with the needs of the business community.

As most accountants freely admit, accounting is more art than science. Many of its concepts have been born of controversy and much of its terminology is imprecise. Witness, for example, the concept of cost as an asset, the interchanging of the terms cost and expense; profit and earnings; revenue, income and sales; and the arbitrary use of the holdover terms debit and credit. In many instances these are hazards that cannot be wished away. The student can only regard them as obstacles to be endured, and mastered, as part of his initiation into the "mysteries" of the art.

Although the accountant routinely resolves most of these matters without direct reference to management, it is well for the manager to be aware of them in interpreting financial data.

Wrong assumptions from a lack of understanding of what is being presented in a financial statement could be more dangerous than not using the statement at all. For this reason some basic principles relating to the accounting function are herewith reviewed.

THE "BUSINESS ENTITY" CONCEPT

The term *business entity* signifies that, from the standpoint of accounting, a business establishment stands as a complete and separate "being." Its affairs are distinct from the personal affairs of the owners and stockholders. Just as the company is given a legal "body," so to speak, when it is incorporated by the state, the company becomes a commercial "body" insofar as business customs and practices are concerned.

Although a proprietorship (unincorporated and owned by one individual) is not a separate entity under the law, it is treated by the accountant as a separate *business* entity. So is a partnership (unincorporated and owned by two or more individuals). Major problems can arise when a proprietor or business partner is compelled to pay creditors from his personal assets in the event of financial failure of the business. While this personal liability does exist for owners of unincorporated business establishments, the accountant keeps business accounts distinct and does not mix personal accounts with them in the financial statements. The business entity concept is further explained in Chapter 10, which describes forms of ownership in some detail.

THE "GOING CONCERN" ASSUMPTION

For purposes of the financial statements, the accountant assumes that the business is a "going concern"—that it is going to continue to operate for an indefinite period of time.

It would be a rare thing for anyone to start a business with the idea of liquidating it soon thereafter. Liquidation is of course possible—through action initiated by the owners or by their creditors—in the event of business failure. Excepting this contingency, it is important to assume a going-concern status because of the inherent effect on valuation of assets and liabilities and on proper recognition of income and expense. This assumption also allows the accountant to assign values—to carry certain assets on the books at cost, for example, and expense them as they are used. A foodservice has many items of equipment and stock that would have little or no value if it suddenly closed its doors, but which have considerable value so long as it remains in operation.

For example: A restaurant has just signed a 12-month lease on a building that can only be used as a restaurant. Assuming the restaurant will continue in operation and receive significant revenue from the use of the building, the lease would be a valuable asset. If, however, the restaurant were suddenly to close, the value of this asset might be reduced to zero. Let us say the restaurant stays in business and buys a new stainless-steel kitchen. Under the going-concern concept the accountant values the kitchen equipment on the basis of its future usefulness in producing income. Next, the restaurant buys menus, place mats and guest checks designed for that particular operation, with the name and address imprinted thereon. The only value these items have depends on continued operation of the restaurant.

In short, the accountant assumes that the business will continue to operate and values its assets accordingly.

PERIODICITY OF ACCOUNTS

A business operation is evaluated with respect to some unit of time. The unit can be a day, week, month, quarter or year, depending on the nature of the activity being evaluated. For example: *daily* sales, *weekly* food purchases and payment of wages, *monthly* payment of rent, *yearly* reckoning of income. Some foodservice operations divide the calendar year into 13 equal periods for accounting purposes, judging that periods having the same number of days, weekends, etc., make for better comparison and control. Other foodservices use the regular calendar year, January through December, or a fiscal year, which could be any 12 consecutive months. However constituted, the business year may be divided into various segments setting forth the periods to be covered by financial statements. For instance, the month may be used as the period for the income & expense statement; the quarter (three months) for the balance sheet; and the twelvemonth for a comprehensive balance sheet, income & expense statement, and other annual accounting.

MATCHING EXPENSE TO INCOME

To show accurately the relation of profit (loss) to sales, it is necessary to consider the expense involved in developing the sales. In doing so the accountant must be careful to charge *all* sales expense, and *only* such expense, against the revenues from those sales. The principle of offsetting expense incurred in the production of income is known as "matching."

Example: During the month of March a foodservice operation has sales of $65,000. Against this income the accountant will charge expenses for food, wages, rent, depreciation, advertising and other operating expenses incurred during the period. If expenses rightly chargeable to another period or operation were to creep into this production account, the profit shown would not be a true figure and any decision based on it would be misguided.

CONSISTENCY IN ACCOUNTING PROCEDURE

There is often more than one right way to do a job. For the accountant the important thing is to do it the same right way every time. Consistency of method is an elementary but critical principle in accounting. This can readily be seen when we consider how much it involves collecting the same kind of data again and again and presenting it at repeated intervals. To be comparable, the ledger entries we make today must be in the same terms as those made yesterday. And the financial statements summarizing these data must be compatible with previous reports if they are to be useful to management, investors, tax authorities and others. Any necessary changes must of course be explained to all concerned.

Consider the application of this

principle in valuating the inventory of a foodservice. Let's suppose that the ABC Foodservice has been using the time-honored system of issuing items from inventory at the purchase price. This would mean that if the foodservice had meat on hand at $1 a pound and received another shipment at $2 a pound, it would first issue the meat at $1 a pound, and when that amount was gone it would start to issue the remainder on hand at the new price of $2 per pound. This is known as the "first-in, first-out" (FIFO) method of pricing inventory. As a further example, assume that the following purchases of the same cut of meat were made in the month of January at the various prices indicated.

Date	Price per Pound	Number of Pounds
Jan. 2	$1.00	20
8	1.25	20
15	1.50	20
22	1.75	20
28	2.00	20

If we price the remaining inventory using the FIFO method it is recognized that the merchandise purchased first was issued first and at the purchase price. This would leave on hand the later purchases. If ending inventory was 25 pounds the inventory value would be:

20 lbs.	@	$2.00	$40.00
5 lbs.	@	1.75	8.75
			$48.75

The cost assigned against income this period for the meat consumed would be:

20 lbs.	@	$1.00	$20.00
20 lbs.	@	1.25	25.00
20 lbs.	@	1.50	30.00
15 lbs.	@	1.75	26.25
Total Cost			$101.25

Let's assume that, because of continually increasing prices, management considered it would be advantageous to change the method of computing inventory to the "last-in, first-out" (LIFO) method of pricing. Using this method all issues would be priced at the price paid for the merchandise purchased last. Merchandise would continue to be issued in the same manner as always, i.e., oldest merchandise issued first, to produce rotation in stock. In the following example, we use the same issues and purchases, and the LIFO ending inventory is:

20 lbs.	@	$1.00	$20.00
5 lbs.	@	1.25	6.25
			$26.25

Cost assigned to the January income statement would be:

15 lbs.	@	$1.25	$18.75
20 lbs.	@	1.50	30.00
20 lbs.	@	1.75	35.00
20 lbs.	@	2.00	40.00
Total Cost			$123.75

Although we have reduced the value of the inventory on the books, we have increased the apparent cost and thereby reduced the profit shown. Since this method of accounting for cost and inventory is accepted by the Internal Revenue Service, many organizations use it. To change the system the accountant would need to receive authority from the I.R.S., and would indicate the change on his financial statements.

Again, consider the importance of using a consistent procedure in figuring depreciation on equipment. For example: On January 2, management bought kitchen equipment at a cost of $10,000. The useful life of the equipment was estimated at 10 years, and this was also in accordance with the depreciation schedules suggested by the Internal Revenue Service. At the end of the 10 years the equipment might still be serviceable but for accounting purposes its total value would have been written off or depreciated, and its value would be zero. Management in this case has made the decision that minimum depreciation should be claimed and so the "straight-line" method of depreciation is applied. The first-year depreciation would be computed by taking one-tenth of the cost. The depreciation claimed for the first year would then be $1,000. For the second through the tenth years the company would continue to claim depreciation expense on this equipment of $1,000.

Management might have elected to depreciate the machine in the same number of years but to claim a larger amount of depreciation in the early years of the life of the machine and a smaller amount in the later years. The "double-declining" method of depreciating the equipment also might have been used. This method would yield first-year depreciation of $2,000 as compared to the $1,000 using the straight-line method. The second year the double-declining method would yield $1,600 depreciation while the straight-line figure would continue to be $1,000. Each year the depreciation claimed, using the double-declining method, would become smaller, while by the straight-line method it would remain the same. Over the 10-year period either method would result in depreciation of the entire $10,000 value of the machine.

As before, it is evident that if it were not for the principle of consistency, the financial statements could be manipulated, substantially altering the financial statements, and unsuspecting statement readers would be led to wrong conclusions.

FULL DISCLOSURE

The accountant is obligated to give a true and complete picture of the financial affairs of the company. Any fact that would affect an appraisal of the organization's financial position and operations must be disclosed in the summary statements issued. For example, these include assets pledged to creditors for security, leases to which the company is pledged, other contingent liabilities, pending court actions, and, as indicated above, any changes in the way the company derives its data and displays it. In fine, any legitimate user of the company's financial reports must be free to assume that appropriate information has been disclosed without reservation.

MONEY AS THE CRITERION OF VALUE

In the exchange of goods and services and in the payment of debts, money is the primary medium of exchange and

historical cost

the measure of value.[1] The accountant records the value of all sales and purchases in terms of money. The value of a purchase is the amount of dollars paid for it. When an item is purchased, a value in terms of dollars—its cost—is assigned to it by the accountant. This amount does not change even though the purchasing power, or value, of the dollar does change. The item is depreciated at the value assigned to it, not at the current market value. The accountant does not take into consideration the changing value of the dollar. He assumes that the dollar remains stable. For example, a foodservice purchases land and a building. The value of the property is its cost in dollars. The value of the property might change, but it is carried on the books at the purchase price. The accountant might be asked by management to render a separate statement showing the increased or decreased market value of the property in terms of the current dollar, but such a comparative statement would not routinely be prepared in most cases.

In recent years the practice of using a stable dollar in recording the value of all sales and purchases has been a subject of controversy in the business and financial world. For years, when the rate of inflation was low, the value of the dollar changed slowly. However, with rapid inflation of dollar values, prices increase drastically and records that once were valid may no longer be realistic.

The problem will likely be ironed out in time, but the difficulties of selecting the base year, and determining a current value of the dollar satisfactory to all business interests, poses a tremendous challenge. To ease the problem some accounting firms provide their customers with supplementary financial statements. These statements may base the dollar value on the price index established for the current year, or they may use a ratio of the current price index to the price index for the year of original record to derive a conversion factor.

OBJECTIVITY IN ACCOUNTING

In rendering statements the accountant must see the foodservice company and its activities from an unemotional and unbiased viewpoint, reporting matters as they really stand, not the way management might wish them to be or in a manner that would tend to distort judgment. Accounting records must be maintained with a high degree of integrity, and the data should be supported with substantial evidence. If the businessperson cannot rely on the information as given, it is very difficult to make good decisions. Investors and creditors likewise have to be sure of the information, or their judgment will be in error. Accounting records should not be used to influence the decision-maker, no matter who it is, but should present a true and clear financial picture of the company.

---

1. A strong case can be made for labor as *the* fundamental measure of the exchangeable value of commodities, as Adam Smith does in his classical treatise *The Wealth of Nations* (Vol. I, Ch. 5). Today money has become the most widely used practical standard.

THE ACCOUNTANT'S CONSERVATIVE TILT

provide for all losses anticipate no gains

To offset a tendency of the enterprising business man or woman to be overoptimistic, accountants tend to be overcautious. They are inclined to think it better to be conservative since the effect of a conservative opinion is not as likely to court disaster as a highly venturesome one. For example, the accountant traditionally makes provisions for projected losses, but does not show projected profits. If reserves have been established for losses that do not occur, the company could only be in the happy position of having funds available for investment or distribution. However, if certain plans have been made based on anticipated profits that did not materialize, the company could be in trouble. Revenue is not recognized until it is earned. Simply because an item appears to have increased in value is not justification for recording an increase. The accountant waits until it has been sold.

THE MATERIALITY OF ERROR

Every bookkeeper is familiar with the nightmare of looking for the lost penny —or the extra one! It is not the penny, but the haunting fear that something *important* is wrong. Precision in accounting is to be desired, but not to the exclusion of everything else. Whether an error, or a fact, is material is a matter of judgment. And there is no hard-and-fast formula. A dollar tip would be material to a waitress. A dollar discrepancy in the cash register might be considered relatively insignificant by management. For a large company the decision to pur-chase equipment costing $25,000 may be a relatively easy one to make. For a small company the same purchase may be the biggest decision management ever made.

Since "to err is human" the accountant may be given some leeway in resolving mistakes that don't make a real difference to the business. If the inclusion or exclusion of a transaction, or an error in posting, has negligible effect on the total statement, the accountant might well be given the latitude of correcting it or noting it and waiving the discrepancy.

INCOME RECOGNITION

There are two basic ways of recognizing income: (1) the cash method; and (2) the accrual method. In cash accounting, income is recognized when payment is received for goods or services. The time of the sale is not the governing factor. The accountant is interested in knowing when cash is received.

In accrual accounting the accountant will recognize income at the time the goods are sold or the service rendered. In this instance the time of receipt of payment is not controlling.

An example will help to show the difference. Assume that on March 28 a customer who has a charge account with the restaurant is served dinner. On March 31 the customer is rendered a statement for the value of the dinner. The customer receives the statement and, in payment, sends a check which arrives at the restaurant on April 15. When will the accountant recognize the income?

1. Under the cash accounting system: Income will be recognized at the time payment is received—April 15. The accountant is not interested in when the service was performed, but when payment was received.
2. Under the accrual accounting system: Income will be recognized when the service was performed—March 28. The deciding factor is not when the money was received, but when the service was performed.

EXPENSE RECOGNITION

The same principle which applies to the recognition of income is applicable to expense. Depending on whether cash or accrual accounting is used, expense is charged at the time cash is paid or when the goods or services are provided. Example: An employee works from March 21 to March 29 and is paid on April 4. When is the expense recognized?

1. Under cash accounting: The accountant recognizes the expense on April 4. It does not matter when the services were performed; the restaurant recognizes the expense when cash is paid.
2. Under accrual accounting: The expense is recognized as an expense for March, the month during which the pay was earned. If the pay period were to extend into April the expense for labor would be charged proportionately to March and April.

SUMMARY

The accountant is guided in his work by certain established principles. These have developed as the accounting profession, in endeavoring to serve the entire business community, found that its efforts would be of little value unless they provided all interested parties with a clear and complete financial picture. The accountant knows that the operating principles by which he is guided must continue to evolve as the needs of business and the society it serves continue to change and grow. These principles have developed from theories and concepts, but have become so firmly entrenched in accounting practice as to have much the same effect as law. A number of principles have been explained, but by no means all, to give the reader at least an introduction to the accountant's task and responsibility. We have reviewed the fundamental concept of the separate and distinct business entity; we have seen that a business is almost always assumed to be a growing entity, and that its future insofar as possible is planned and premeasured.

We have further seen that there is a predictable rhythm in the way it analyzes and projects its financial operations, and that there must be a corresponding regularity and logic in its accounting methods. The accountant, we recognize, must report fully and dispassionately, with a sense of hard reality rather than adventure, and must take care to apply universally adopted standards of value to make his reports meaningful to a variety of users inside the company and beyond.

STUDY QUESTIONS

1. List three groups, other than management, that have a valid interest in the financial statements of a foodservice company.

2. Explain why one or more of these non-managerial groups would be concerned with adherence to the principles of *consistency* and *full disclosure* in accounting practice.

3. Describe the concept of "business entity."

4. Explain briefly why the "going-concern" principle has a basic significance for the accountant.

5. Name the two methods of accounting for income and expense, and explain how they operate.

6. Why might a company want to change the method of accounting for depreciation?

7. As you see it, what have been the self-interest motives on the part of business people which have compelled them to follow standard accounting concepts and practices? Discuss briefly.

8. With regard to your discussion in 7 above, distinguish between the working of voluntary rules and statutory law as seen in the "business entity" concept applied to proprietorships versus the "legal entity" status of corporations.

PART TWO
WHAT ACCOUNTING TELLS THE MANAGER

CHAPTER 4

FINANCIAL STATEMENTS

Windows on the statics and dynamics of a business

PURPOSE

To examine the function of the fundamental accounting statements—the *balance sheet* and the *income & expense statement;* and to see how these statements satisfy the interests of management, investors and creditors in evaluating the financial position and the profit potential of a business enterprise.

CONTENT

Role of the Income & Expense Statement and the Balance Sheet

Structure of the Income Statement
    Sales
    Controllable expense
    Profit before occupation costs
    Occupation costs
    Profit before depreciation
    Depreciation

Structure of the Balance Sheet
    Assets
    Liabilities
    Owners' equity
    When rendered
    The accounting equation

The Interrelationship of Financial Statements

ALMOST ALL BUSINESS ORGANIZATIONS, whether proprietorships, partnerships, or corporations—regardless of the product or service—use two basic accounting statements: the *balance sheet* and the *income & expense statement* (sometimes called simply the *income statement*).

The balance sheet is a statement of financial position[1] at a particular time, which demonstrates that balance has been kept between assets on one side and liabilities and capital on the other side of the accounting equation. The income & expense statement shows the total revenue and expenses for a specified period of operations.[2]

Both of these basic financial statements result from the normal flow of accounting data common to every business. As seen in Exhibit 4–1, they serve as receptacles for totals arrived at when various categories of revenue and expense are summarized. Both contain information of vital concern to management, but their use often suffers from lack of understanding of the story they tell.

The profit (or loss) figure at the foot of the income & expense statement derives from a comparison of revenues and expenses occurring during the operating period covered. This is the familiar "bottom line" that business people are so interested in. There is certainly no criticism to be made of watching the bottom

line. In foodservice operations, especially, it is important to do so. The frequency with which this statement is rendered will vary from a week to a year. During critical periods—as when a major menu change has been made some operators may even ask for this report daily. Generally speaking it is considered essential on at least an annual basis (see Exhibits 4–2 and 4–3).

The important thing for the manager to know about the bottom line, aside from the color of the ink and the size of the number, is how the bottom line figure came to be what it is. That's what statement analysis is all about, as we will begin to see more clearly in the following chapter, and in a very real sense this is what financial management comes down to.

If the income statement tells us *how* we got where we are, the balance sheet tells us *where* we are at any given time. Again, if the income statement may be likened to a motion picture of the operation, the balance sheet is like a snapshot at a fixed point in time. In other words, the balance sheet shows what is owned and what is owed by the company, and accounts for the difference. It may be rendered on a monthly basis, but in many small activities it is rendered on a quarterly or annual basis. This statement reflects the financial condition of the company and not the profitability of the company's operation (see Exhibits 4–4 and 4–5).

Both the income statement and the balance sheet are important to manage-

---

1. And is so called in more formal terms.
2. And also known as the profit and loss statement.

ment in its decision-making role. These statements may be used individually or together, as will be indicated in the next chapter. Since the income statement tells the amount of sales, expenses and net profit (or loss), it is of foremost operational significance. To assist management in controlling operations, the income statement should be prepared as soon as possible after the fiscal period covered. This is necessary to allow a quick exam-

ination of the profitability of the company's activities. If there are expenses out of line, or if earnings are not in keeping with budget projections, immediate corrections can be made. In this manner the income statement helps to operate the business in an efficient and profitable manner.

The balance sheet, with its information about the company's assets and their relationship to liabilities and owners'

THE FLOW OF ACCOUNTING

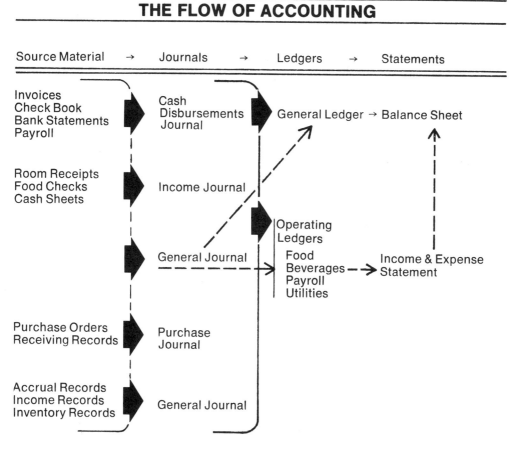

EXHIBIT 4-1   Another look at the accounting flow, showing how income data feeds into the balance sheet.

equity, is of interest to purveyors, investors, and creditors, as well as the owners. The kind of assets the company has, whether they are easily converted into cash, and the nature of its indebtedness, whether long- or short-term, will determine the solvency of the company. The company could be showing a profit and still find difficulty meeting its obligations if its funds have not been wisely handled.

The foodservice operator may answer many questions using these two basic statements, and comparing them with previous ones. For example:

—How profitable is the business?

—Are the profits providing the owners with sufficient return on their investment?

—Is there sufficient income to pay expenses?

—Is there enough cash on hand?

—What should the future hold, based on past performance?

To illustrate the use of these statements, let us consider some practical examples.

THE INCOME & EXPENSE STATEMENT

Exhibit 4–2 is an income statement for the ABC Foodservice Company. This is an annual statement summarizing all income and expense. It will be noted that the first item shown is sales, which is understood to be revenue, or income, from sales. The amount shown is a cumulative total for one year.

ABC Foodservice Company, Inc.
INCOME & EXPENSE STATEMENT
Year Ending Dec. 31, 19xx

Sales		$100,000.00
Less: Cost of Goods Sold		35,000.00
Gross Profit		65,000.00
Controllable Expenses		
Payroll	33,000.00	
Operating Expenses	10,000.00	
Total	43,000.00	
Occupation Costs	8,000.00	
Total Operating Expense and Occupancy Costs		51,000.00
Net Income		$14,000.00

EXHIBIT 4–2   An income statement in gross figures, as often seen in corporate reports.

The rest of the items on the statement, except for net income, are expenses incurred in earning income. The net income, or profit, is the residual which may eventually go to the owner of the restaurant. Expenses are broken down into several categories, representing major expenses necessary to produce income.

The first expense classification indicated is the cost of goods sold. This is the actual cost of food used to prepare the meals served. Subtracting the cost of food from the sales figure gives us gross profit. Gross profit is the amount left to meet payroll, rent, other operating expenses, taxes, interest, depreciation, and the like. In our example we assume that the restaurant is selling food only. If it were also selling beverages there would be another sales line for this, and the cost of goods sold would also be divided into separate categories for food and beverages.[3]

Separate food and beverage accounting allows for proper evaluation of each operation, and is important even if these operations are managed by the same person. Assume, for example, that a food-service operation is making higher-than-average profits in beverage sales and lower-than-average profits in food sales. Unless the figures are treated separately the profit figure would be an average of the two, and it would appear that a good job was being done in both departments.

The next category on our statement is Controllable expenses. These expenses are so designated because management

does have a measure of control over them. Payroll expense, for instance, can be controlled by managing the size of the work force.

Operating expenses include other controllable expenses, such as linen and laundry, tableware, cleaning materials, and paper supplies. Advertising, utilities, administrative and maintenance expense might also be covered by this category. Although generally classified as controllable, pay of personnel is subject to wage contracts, the labor market, and other factors beyond the direct influence of management.

Occupation costs are largely uncontrollable. This category includes rent, property taxes, insurance, interest, and depreciation. Interest on notes payable, for example, depends upon the amount of money borrowed, and depreciation on equipment depends on the cost of the equipment, rather than the volume of sales. Furthermore, the lease on a building, the depreciation rate established for equipment and the interest on a capital improvement loan usually commit management for long periods.

As the business becomes larger and the management task more complex, more is demanded of the accounting statements. A look at Exhibit 4–3 will show immediately that this has been the case with ABC Foodservice Company. The form of this income & expense statement follows the form recommended by the *Uniform System of Accounts for Restaurants*. It will be noted that the statement not only shows the information in greater detail but also expresses each entry as a percentage. Most statements that satisfy the needs of government and management are good state-

---

3. See Chapter 9, Exhibit 9–2. Although this is an example of a budget, it indicates how sales and cost of sales are handled when both food and beverages are sold.

ments. However, for decision-making and comparative study a statement not only must show a substantial amount of information, but must show it in a way that conforms to the presentation method used by similar companies.

ABC Foodservice Company

INCOME & EXPENSE STATEMENT

Year Ending Dec. 31, 19xx

	Amount	Percent
TOTAL SALES	$1,605,995	100.0%
Cost of Sales		
Food (after credit for employee meals)	555,402	34.6
Gross Profit	1,050,593	65.4
Other Income	0	0
Total Income	$1,050,593	65.4%
Controllable Expenses		
Payroll	477,284	29.7
Employee benefits	39,667	2.5
Direct operating expenses	73,849	4.6
Music and entertainment	—	
Advertising and promotion	911	.1
Utilities	30,374	1.9
Administrative and general	192,630	12.0
Repairs and maintenance	24,486	1.5
Total Controllable Expenses	$ 839,201	52.3%
Income before Rent or Occupation Costs	211,392	13.1
Occupation Costs		
Rent or occupation costs	$ 140,723	8.7
Depreciation	46,628	2.9
Income Tax	11,794	.7
Total Occupation Costs	$ 199,145	12.3%
NET PROFIT	$ 12,247	0.8%

EXHIBIT 4–3   A more detailed income statement, giving percentages as well as dollar figures.

THE BALANCE SHEET

Exhibit 4–4 is an example of the balance sheet of a typical foodservice establishment. It is a statement showing the exact condition of the business as of December 31. It does not tell how profitable the business was during the past year, but it does tell how much the company owns, how much of what it owns is obligated to creditors and how much is obligated to owners, at year's end. We know from our discussion in Chapter 2 that liabilities plus owners' equity must equal assets, so let us examine the accounts on this balance sheet to see how we arrive at the totals and how they keep the equation in balance.

Assets are shown in the first grouping of accounts on the balance sheet. The reader will note that there are two general classifications of assets, current assets and fixed assets. Current assets may be defined as assets which are in the form of cash or which will be converted into cash or consumed in the near future, usually in one year or less. Included in the category of current assets are cash, accounts receivable, inventory and prepaid expenses.

Cash is by definition a current asset. We treat accounts receivable under current assets because these accounts represent money collectable in the near future. Inventory is classified as a current asset because inventory is expected to be used up in the near future. It is intended, for instance, that the food we have in inventory will be served to customers within a year. Prepaid expenses include such things as advance payment on a lease, insurance premiums paid in advance, or other things that have already been paid for and will be used in the current operating period.

The other general classification, fixed assets, embraces assets that have a long life and will produce revenue over many accounting periods. These assets are sometimes called "plant assets." They include land, buildings, furniture and fixtures, kitchen equipment, leasehold improvements and other property with a useful life extending beyond a year. Exhibit 4–4 lists land and a building. The value shown for the building has been reduced by an account called accumulated depreciation. Accumulated depreciation is an account showing the amount of decline in value of a fixed asset. The balance sheet shows that we paid $15,000 for the building. Since we bought the building it has been depreciated by $8,000. The remaining value on our books is $7,000. This $7,000 figure may not represent the market value of the building but is the remaining portion of the cost which is yet to be systematically written off over its expected useful life.

The second major grouping of accounts on the balance sheet covers liabilities. From our definition of liabilities we know that these accounts indicate the things we owe. The liabilities group is broken down into two classifications: (1) current liabilities; and (2) long-term liabilities. Current liabilities are those debts which come due and must be paid within a year. Long-term liabilities are debts which will mature later than one year from the date of the balance sheet.

Let us now examine each of the current liabilities shown in Exhibit 4–4. Accounts payable includes all those things for which we owe in the normal course of business, such as inventory, electric

ABC Foodservice Company

BALANCE SHEET

December 31, 19xx

ASSETS

Current Assets

Cash	$21,000
Accounts Receivable	3,000
Inventory	6,000
Prepaid Expenses	3,000
Total Current Assets	33,000

Fixed Assets

Land		5,000	
Building	15,000		
Less: Accumulated Depreciation	8,000	7,000	
Total Fixed Assets			12,000
TOTAL ASSETS			$45,000

LIABILITIES AND CAPITAL

Liabilities

Current Liabilities

Accounts Payable	4,000	
Notes Payable—Current Portion	5,000	
Accrued Liabilities	1,000	
Total Current Liabilities		10,000

Long-Term Liabilities

Notes Payable—Long-Term Portion	15,000
Total Liabilities	25,000

Capital

Joe Jones, Capital	20,000
TOTAL LIABILITIES AND CAPITAL	$45,000

EXHIBIT 4–4   A balance sheet typical of a one-owner establishment.

ABC Foodservice Company, Inc.
BALANCE SHEET
Dec. 31, 19xx

Current Assets

Cash and Securities	$116,273
Accounts Receivable (less Allowances)	3,164
Inventories	23,297
Prepaid Expenses	27,279
Total Current Assets	$170,013

Long-Term Assets

Due from Stockholders	—
Property, Plant & Equipment (less Depreciation)	304,108
Goodwill	18,578
TOTAL ASSETS	$492,699

Current Liabilities

Accounts Payable	$ 93,857
Accrued Taxes	12,103
Accrued Wages, Interest	2,950
Total Current Liabilities	$108,910

Long-Term Liabilities

Due to Stockholders	34,648
Chattel Mortgages Due	148,237
Other Mortgages Due	10,000
Total Long-Term Liabilities	192,885
Total Liabilities	$301,795

Stockholders' Equity

Common Stock—1,000 shares authorized. 4,270 Outstanding	42,740
Retained Earnings	148,164
Total Stockholders' Equity	$190,904
TOTAL LIABILITIES AND STOCKHOLDERS' EQUITY	$492,699

EXHIBIT 4–5 A typical corporation balance sheet.

service, advertising and supplies. The designation notes payable—current portion is the amount payable within the next 12 months on outstanding loans. In our example this totals $5,000. Accrued liabilities are debts for which the company has not been invoiced. This line includes such items as wages for the last few days of the month that are not paid until the first of the next month, and a property tax assessment which has not been billed.

The other major classification of liabilities is long-term liabilities. Our example shows only the long-term portion of notes payable, totaling $15,000. The current liabilities section showed $5,000 in notes payable. The two accounts combined indicate $20,000 is owed on notes payable—$5,000 due in the next 12 months and $15,000 due after 12 months.

The difference between accounts payable and notes payable is primarily a legal difference. Accounts payable are accounts owed to general creditors. They do not involve a signed legal document as is the case with notes payable.

The capital section of our balance sheet shows that Joe Jones, owner of the ABC Foodservice Company, has a net worth of $20,000.

The total assets in our balance sheet are thus shown to equal total liabilities plus capital, and the statement is in balance $(A = L + C)$.

OWNERSHIP GOES PUBLIC

Exhibit 4–5 indicates further growth in the company. But something else has also changed. To achieve the desired growth it was apparently necessary for Mr. Jones to change the form of ownership of the

ABC FOODSERVICE COMPANY

COMPARATIVE STATEMENTS
Trial Balance, Balance Sheet, Profit and Loss Statement

	Adjusted Trial Balance End of Year	
Cash and Securities	$ 116,273	
Accounts Receivable Less Reserve	3,164	
Inventories	23,297	
Prepaid Expenses	27,279	
Due from Stockholders		
Property, Plant & Equip. Less Depr.	304,108	
Goodwill	18,578	
Accounts Payable		$ 93,857
Accrued Taxes		12,103
Accrued Wages, Interest		2,950
Due to Stockholders		34,648
Chattel Mortgages Due		148,237
Other Mortgages Due		10,000
Common Stock		42,740
Retained Earnings		105,521
Sales		1,605,995
Other Income		30,396
Cost of Food	555,402	
Cost of Administration	3,320	
Cost of Wages	477,284	
Cost of Rent	130,888	
Maintenance, Repairs, Replacements	24,486	
Cost of Utilities	30,374	
Cost of Advertising	911	
Cost of Warehousing	53,422	
Taxes — Employee, State & Federal	39,667	
Laundry — Uniforms	18,068	
Office and Miscellaneous	4,187	
Professional Fees	16,915	
Insurance	38,208	
Officers' Salaries	130,000	
Depreciation	46,628	
Automobile Expense	2,359	
Interest Charges	9,835	
Taxes — Federal Income	11,794	
TOTALS	$2,086,447	$2,086,447
Net Income		

EXHIBIT 4–6   A report showing the interrelation of basic financial statements.

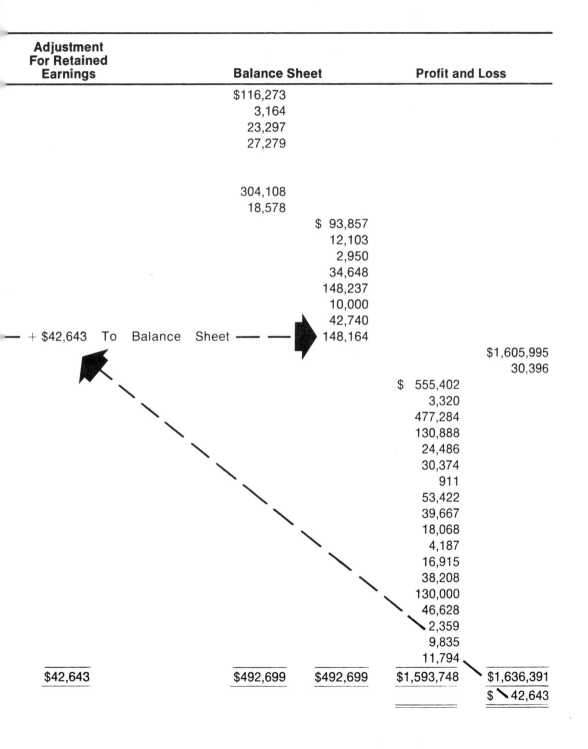

Adjustment For Retained Earnings	Balance Sheet		Profit and Loss	
	$116,273			
	3,164			
	23,297			
	27,279			
	304,108			
	18,578			
		$ 93,857		
		12,103		
		2,950		
		34,648		
		148,237		
		10,000		
		42,740		
+ $42,643 To Balance Sheet		148,164		
				$1,605,995
				30,396
			$ 555,402	
			3,320	
			477,284	
			130,888	
			24,486	
			30,374	
			911	
			53,422	
			39,667	
			18,068	
			4,187	
			16,915	
			38,208	
			130,000	
			46,628	
			2,359	
			9,835	
			11,794	
$42,643	$492,699	$492,699	$1,593,748	$1,636,391
				$ 42,643

company and its legal status. The proprietorship has become a corporation. The corporation has sold stock and now the capital section of the statement has become shareholders' equity. Since in a corporation the profits may either be distributed to the collective owners as dividends on their shares, or be reinvested in the business, a new account comes into the picture, retained earnings. The accumulated profits of the corporation will be retained in this account until management has decided if they should be distributed to the shareholders or used for other purposes.

Using the *corporate* records of the ABC Foodservice Company, Exhibit 4–6 shows the trial balance, which has been prepared from the totals accumulated in the various ledger accounts. With the exception of the retained earnings account all accounts have been adjusted where necessary (for instance: deferred or prepaid expenses, accrued expenses, deferred or accrued income, payroll taxes, and overage or shortage in inventory). The income & expense statement is completed and the net income has been established for the year. At this time the undistributed profit would be added to the retained earnings and held in that account for final disposition by management. With this adjustment the balance sheet can now be completed. (Exhibits 4–3 and 4–5 show the completed income & expense statement and the balance sheet for the corporation in their final form. A comparison of these and previous statements will show the reader how the figures have been derived.) As indicated in Exhibit 4–6, the net income, which becomes the adjustment for retained earnings, is the link between the income & expense statement and the balance sheet.

SUMMARY

Two accounting statements are fundamental to the foodservice company: the *balance sheet* and the *income & expense statement* (or simply the *income statement*). Each of these statements provides management with a specific kind of information. They serve as receptacles for a flow of detailed accounting data, organizing these data into summaries that tell the manager where the business stands and how it got there.

The balance sheet lists the total assets, liabilities and capital of the company at a specific point in time, and in so doing balances the two sides of the accounting equation: $A = L + C$. Assets (A) on the left side represent all equity and must equal the total of liabilities (L; creditors' equity) and capital (C; owners' equity) on the right side of the equation. The balance sheet is usually prepared monthly but may be drawn up at less frequent intervals—at the end of a quarter, a six-month period, or a year.

The income statement summarizes activities of the company for a selected operating period—in terms of sales, revenues derived from sales, and expenses incurred in making sales—and shows the resulting profit or loss. This statement reflects the manager's ability to manage and is often used to evaluate the efficiency of operations as well as to indicate how large and profitable they have been. This statement is rendered very close to the end of the period covered, often monthly, so that the manager has current information on which to act.

The balance sheet, the income statement and other financial reports provide information to interests outside the company as well as to its owners and managers. Government agencies are interested for tax purposes and for economic analyses. Lending institutions have a valid claim on these reports to determine how secure their money will be, and purveyors to determine whether they should extend credit. These and other interested groups will study the statements before entering into financial arrangements with the company.

STUDY QUESTIONS

1. What is the primary purpose of the balance sheet? In a few words describe its relation to the fundamental accounting equation.

2. What is the primary purpose of the income & expense statement? What is the essential difference between this statement and the balance sheet, with respect to what it tells about the company?

3. How often would the accountant normally render a balance sheet for a medium-sized foodservice company?

4. Discuss briefly the timing problem found by the accountant in drawing up an income statement.

5. What outside interests have a valid claim on the information provided in a company's financial statements? List three such groups and explain their interest in general terms.

6. State the general rule for distinguishing between *current assets* and *fixed assets*.

7. Explain how the net income figure links the income statement and the balance sheet.

8. What aspect of occupation costs renders them largely uncontrollable?

CHAPTER 5

STATEMENT ANALYSIS

Measuring sticks used by the accountant

PURPOSE

To discover how the accountant integrates data from the financial statements to produce an array of business measuring devices for management; specifically, to demonstrate the use of various ratios and percentages developed from figures presented in the balance sheet and the income & expense statement and their supporting schedules.

CONTENT

The Tools of Analysis: Ratios, Percentages, Turnover Rates

Liquidity Ratios
    The current ratio
    The quick ratio

Working Capital and the Working Capital Ratio

Leverage Ratios
    Debt-to-equity ratio
    Debt-to-assets ratio

Activity Ratios
    Inventory turnover
    Accounts receivable turnover

Profitability Ratios
    Rate of return on assets
    Rate of return on sales
    Rate of return on owners' equity

THE FINANCIAL STATEMENTS—the balance sheet, the income statement, the statement of retained earnings, and the statement of change in financial position—are not doing their job unless they are fully analyzed. All too frequently, especially in smaller companies, financial statements are prepared by the accountant and little or no use is made of the information they contain. Consider the case in which these statements are used only to file the required tax returns. If the accountant's work is only used for this purpose, much of its value is being wasted. These statements should be carefully interpreted and used by management to make financial decisions.

Almost every decision management makes has some effect on the financial condition of the company. Management must have accurate and timely information to know whether to buy or lease equipment, change hours of operation, add to or reduce the size of staff, among the dozens of decisions that require daily and almost minute-by-minute attention. Although these decisions often prove to be good, the predictability of success is much greater when they are based on the best possible information.

Reliable accounting information is not in itself a guarantee that management will make correct decisions. Sometimes the managers of large businesses make decisions for which they have complete and accurate accounting information and still find the decisions to be wrong and costly to the company. Even though managers can make bad business decisions with good information, in the long run it is much more difficult to make good decisions with bad information than it is to make good decisions with good information. Good accounting data increases the probability that managers will make correct decisions, assuming they interpret the data correctly.

With these observations on the importance of good accounting information, let us examine carefully the various methods used. Our discussion will divide the methods of analysis into three categories: (1) ratios; (2) percentages; (3) turnovers.

As we know, a *ratio* is a comparison of two numbers and may be expressed in words or figures. If there were four chairs at each table we would say the ratio of chairs to tables is four to one, 4:1, or 4/1.

Since many proportions are stated with 100 as the base number, it is useful to express a business ratio as a *percentage*. Thus, if we pay back a dollar and a tenth ($1.10) for every dollar borrowed, we say the rate of interest is 10 percent. Or, back to the dining room, the 4:1 ratio of chairs to tables might also be expressed as a percentage: The number of chairs (4) is 400 percent of the number of tables (1).

Turnover, as applied in the restaurant business, generally refers to frequency of use or change. If, on a given night, a table was used four times, we would say the table had a turnover of four. Inventory used up 10 times in a year would be said to have a turnover of 10.

RATIOS IN ACTION

Many different professions use ratios to express relationships which hold fairly constant. A college might hold the student-to-professor ratio at 30:1. The medical profession is concerned with keeping the ratio of patients to physicians as low as possible. Motorists are keen about the ratio between the amount of gas used and the number of miles covered. A hotel is interested in the ratio between the number of rooms and the number of maids it must hire. In a restaurant operation the number of tables to the number of waiters and waitresses required is an operating ratio of prime importance. Let us assume that our restaurant has 60 tables and 10 waitresses. If management wanted to establish the ratio of tables to waitresses it could do so with some simple arithmetic, as follows:

$$\frac{\text{Number of tables}}{\text{Number of waitresses}} = \frac{60}{10} = \frac{6}{1} \text{ or } 6:1$$

The ratios with which we work in business usually fall into one of four classifications: (1) liquidity ratios; (2) leverage ratios; (3) activity ratios or turnover; (4) profitability or rate-of-return ratios.

LIQUIDITY RATIOS

Liquidity measures the ability of the company to pay its debts as they become due. To say that a company has $50,000 with which to pay bills tells us nothing about its liquidity unless we know how much it owes or is likely to owe. It is *relative* cash we are interested in, and the liquidity ratio expresses this fact in a simple, usable form.

The Current Ratio. The most common liquidity ratio is the *current ratio*, the ratio between current assets and current liabilities. As a general rule, a good current ratio is 2 to 1, or $2 of current assets for every $1 of current liabilities. Many foodservice companies operating with cash sales, low inventories (buying on a day-to-day or week-to-week basis) and little if any accounts receivable, believe a 1:1 current ratio is sufficient.

The current ratio can be determined from the statement of current assets and current liabilities in the balance sheet. It will be recalled from the previous chapter that current assets are cash assets or assets which can be converted into cash within the next year, and assets which will be consumed within the year. Current liabilities are those obligations of the company which must be paid within one year. For example: The ABC Company has current assets of $50,000 and current liabilities of $20,000. Its current ratio is 2.5:1, derived by dividing current assets by current liabilities, as follows:

$$\frac{\text{Current Assets}}{\text{Current Liabilities}} = \frac{50,000}{20,000} \text{ or } 2.5:1$$

To say that our company has a 2.5:1 current ratio means that for every $1 of current obligations, the company has $2.50 worth of current assets which can be used to pay those obligations. Assuming that a current ratio of 2:1 is adequate, our company obviously has a better than average liquidity position.

We must not conclude that the ABC Company is in good financial position merely because it has a current ratio above what is generally acceptable. The current ratio only *indicates* that under normal circumstances the company should be able to pay off current debts as they come due.

Assume for instance that the company has a current ratio of 2.5:1 as previously calculated. And suppose that the company has been losing $15,000 per month. If the company continues to operate on this basis it will sooner or later use up all of its cash and other current assets. So the current ratio is a valid measurement of the company's liquidity only if used in conjunction with other applicable measuring sticks.

The Quick Ratio. The *quick ratio*, sometimes referred to as the *acid-test ratio*, is used to determine the company's ability to pay its debts as they come due with regard to very-short-term indebtedness. It is computed as follows:

$$\text{Quick Ratio} = \frac{\text{Current Assets} - \text{Inventory}}{\text{Current Liabilities}}$$

The only difference between the current ratio and the quick ratio is inventory. In the numerator of the current ratio, *all* current assets are used. In the numerator of the quick ratio, current assets minus inventory is used. In the quick ratio, one is trying to measure the firm's ability to pay debts that mature in the very near future. Some industries require considerable time to convert inventories into cash. For them,

the quick ratio would probably be a more appropriate test of liquidity than it would be for the restaurant industry, which has a faster turnover of inventory.

Since inventories are not always a very liquid asset—quickly converted into cash—and since we must keep some inventory in stock for current customers, inventory should not be depleted to pay debts.

Back to our example, let's suppose that current liabilities are still $20,000 and that the current assets of $50,000 break down as follows:

Cash	$10,000
Accounts Receivable	10,000
Inventory	30,000
Total	$50,000

Reasoning that inventories will not be converted into cash to pay bills, we compute the quick ratio as follows:

$$\text{Quick ratio} = \frac{\$50,000 - \$30,000}{\$20,000}$$

$$\text{Quick ratio} = \frac{\$20,000}{\$20,000} \text{ or } 1:1$$

By eliminating inventory as a liquid asset we have determined that for every $1 of current assets we have $1 of current liabilities. This says that if we were required to pay all current debts we would have enough quick assets to do so.

WORKING CAPITAL RATIO

Working capital is not in itself a ratio, but is an essential factor in determining liquidity. It is derived as follows:

Working Capital

= Current Assets − Current Liabilities

As you will note, working capital is simply the excess of current assets over current liabilities. These figures are given in the balance sheet. In our example, current assets were $50,000 and current liabilities were $20,000. Therefore, working capital is $30,000 ($50,000 − $20,000). This tells us the absolute number of dollars the company has to work with, but does not say whether it is enough. Knowing the amount of working capital becomes useful when joined with other information. For example, in a small company $30,000 might be sufficient to support any foreseeable business volume, but in a company that did a much bigger volume of sales, this amount could be wiped out in a very short time. The missing factor in the bare working capital figure, then, is a number relating to sales activity. This is what the *working capital ratio* provides.

The working capital ratio indicates the number of dollars in sales each dollar in working capital generates. The formula is:

$$\text{Working Capital Ratio} = \frac{\text{Net Sales}}{\text{Net Working Capital}}$$

The figures for net sales and net working capital are found in the income statement and the balance sheet, respectively. Knowing our net working capital and finding that net sales were $150,000, the ratio would be:

$$\text{Working Capital Ratio} = \frac{\$150,000}{30,000} = 5:1$$

This means that every $1 of working capital produces $5 in sales. A 5:1 working capital ratio could indicate a fairly good relationship. *Too* large a ratio could indicate inadequate working capital, while too small a ratio would indicate that working capital was not being put to good use and might be invested with better results elsewhere.

LEVERAGE RATIOS

In a variety of ways, leverage ratios measure owners' equity against creditors' equity. All of the assets of the company have claims against them either by creditors (in the form of liabilities) or by owners (in the form of owners' equity or capital). In other words, *leverage ratios* compare what the company owns to what it owes. Let's examine some of the more common leverage ratios.

Debt-to-Equity Ratio. The *debt-to-equity ratio* compares total creditors' claims to owners' claims. It is stated as follows:

$$\frac{\text{Current Liabilities} + \text{Long-term Liabilities}}{\text{Owners' Equity (Capital)}}$$

$$= \frac{\text{Total Liabilities}}{\text{Owners' Equity}}$$

This ratio expresses the relation between the number of creditor dollars the company has been able to use and the number of dollars the owners have invested in the company.

Suppose the company has current liabilities of $10,000 and long-term liabilities of $20,000. Adding the current liabilities and long-term liabilities, we have total liabilities of $30,000. Assume that the amount invested by the owners (owners' equity) is $20,000. The debt-to-equity ratio is as follows:

$$\frac{\$30,000}{\$20,000} = 1.5:1$$

This says that for every $1 the owners have put into the company, they are using $1.50 of creditors' money. The company "uses" creditors' money by buying merchandise on account or buying a building or fixed equipment with a mortgage loan. This ratio is important in determining whether the foodservice is using too much credit.

A major cause of failure by the small business is undercapitalization. If owners do not put enough of their own money into the company they will have to go to outside sources for financing. And there is a danger they will become burdened with heavy note payments and find that much of their working capital is used to retire debt. During a slow month this may cause them to be delinquent in other accounts, which would further complicate their cash-flow position.

Debt-to-Assets Ratio. The ratio of total debts to total assets, or debt-to-assets ratio, indicates the percentage of total assets financed by creditors. If total assets of the company are $100,000, and its total debt is $90,000, the debt-to-assets ratio, expressed as a percentage, would be:

$$\text{Debt-to-Assets Ratio} = \frac{\text{Total Liabilities}}{\text{Total Assets}}$$
$$= \frac{\$90,000}{\$100,000}$$
$$= 90\%$$

In most cases such a high percentage of debt financing would indicate we have overextended our credit.

In another example, let us say our total debts are $10,000 and total assets are $100,000. Then:

$$\text{Debt-to-Assets Ratio} = \frac{\text{Total Liabilities}}{\text{Total Assets}}$$
$$= \frac{\$10,000}{\$100,000}$$
$$= 10\%$$

This ratio tells management that 10 percent of the firm's assets have been financed by using debt. The company has made a limited use of other people's money and would most likely be able to weather a few bad months easily. The monthly installment on a $10,000 note, for example, would probably not be too heavy a burden.

Liquidity, solvency and leverage are closely interrelated, as we can see from our discussions of ratios and percentages. Liquidity refers mainly to the amount of working capital or "quick assets" a company has. Solvency is a measure of its ability to pay debts. And leverage compares owners' investment with creditors' "investment," which tells us to what degree nonowners' money is being used by the company.

You might ask why we use other people's money. There are a number of reasons. One of the prime reasons is that the owners may not have sufficient cash to finance a business on their own. And analysis will often show that the owners can make more profit on the dollars they borrow from the bank than they will have to pay the bank in interest.

Another reason for borrowing money is to expand the business. For example, let's assume it takes $50,000 to launch the enterprise. Suppose the owner has $50,000 in cash to finance it. If the owner financed the operation entirely, using no borrowed funds, he would be able to operate one restaurant. An alternate plan would be for him to borrow $25,000 to open the restaurant, using only $25,000 of his own money. After opening this restaurant he would still have $25,000 of his own money. With this $25,000 he could go back to the bank, notify them he still has additional capital and would like to borrow $25,000 more. With this second $25,000 plus his remaining $25,000 he would be able to open a second restaurant.

Another reason for using credit is that in some cases it is a customary and convenient way to do business. Sometimes we will use the credit a supplier routinely grants because the cost of the credit is already incorporated in the price and would not cost anything extra. If by utilizing this credit we find we have extra cash available, we can put this cash in the bank or other interest-bearing account. Without this available cash, we might even have to go to the bank and borrow money to pay a debt that fell due.

ACTIVITY RATIO OR TURNOVER

Activity ratios, as their name implies, measure the activity of a company in some specific area. An activity ratio might be applied to inventory, measuring the number of times we convert inventory into sales. This ratio might also be used to measure the activity in accounts receivable—the time it takes to convert accounts receivable into cash. Let's look at some activity ratios in further detail.

Inventory Turnover. We are usually interested in how many times our inventory turns over in a year. Assume we have an inventory that cost $10,000, and the cost of sales is $10,000 per month or $120,000 per year. We would determine the annual turnover rate as follows:

$$\text{Inventory Turnover} = \frac{\text{Cost of Sales}}{\text{Inventory}}$$
$$= \frac{\$120,000}{\$10,000}$$
$$= 12 \text{ times per yr.}$$

Inventory Turnover tells us that we convert our inventory into sales 12 times a year. Saying it another way, the average unit in inventory is purchased, sold and repurchased 12 times throughout the year. Since the primary activity of the company is buying merchandise to be resold to the consumer, we are of course concerned about the number of times we can convert our inventory into sales. If we turned over inventory only once a year, we would have to make an extremely large profit on each sale. If we turned it over 20 times a year we could make a very narrow margin of profit on each sale and still have an acceptable net income at the end of the year.

Example: In Company A we make one sale per month of $10,000. The cost of the item is $9,000, so on each sale we make $1,000, a substantial profit. In Company B we sell units at $1 each and the cost per unit is $.95. Company B only makes $.05 on each product it sells, and to make $1,000 per month gross profit would have to sell 20,000 units per month. If Company A sells one unit per month, and Company B sells 20,000 units per month, they each make $1,000 per month gross profit. The nature of the foodservice industry is such that it requires a high inventory turnover.

Accounts Receivable Turnover. Accounts receivable turnover is the ratio of credit sales to accounts receivable. Again, we are usually interested in knowing the number of times accounts receivable are converted into cash each year. If the operation sells its products on credit, the cycle involves purchasing merchandise for resale, selling the merchandise on account, purchasing additional merchandise to replace the inventory sold, collecting cash from the customers, selling the merchandise to customers, replacing the merchandise sold to the new customers, and so on. The part of the cycle that concerns us now is the conversion of the accounts receivable into cash. The formula is:

$$\text{Accounts Receivable Turnover} = \frac{\text{Total Credit Sales}}{\text{Accounts Receivable, Average Balance}}$$

Assuming an average accounts receivable of $15,000 and total annual credit sales of $150,000, the turnover rate would be 10 times a year. This tells us that a typical sale is made and collected 10 times throughout the year.

Knowing this turnover rate and the number of days in a year, we can go an additional step and compute the average number of days it takes for a customer to pay his account, as follows:

$$\begin{aligned} \text{Average Days to Collect} &= \frac{360 \text{ days}}{\text{Accounts Receivable Turnover}} \\ &= \frac{360}{10} \\ &= 36 \text{ days} \end{aligned}$$

Thus we find that it takes the average customer 36 days to pay his account. We do not know if this is good, bad or average until we analyze our terms of sale. If payment for credit sales is due 10 days from the date of sale and the average customer takes 36 days to pay, our collections are too slow. Management must try to determine why customers are slow in paying and take appropriate action. If the terms of sale are 30 days, we are only slightly over the desirable collection rate and probably no corrective action is necessary. If the credit terms are 60 days and it takes an average of only 36 days to collect, the collection rate is highly favorable.

The collection rate is important for two reasons: (1) the older an account gets, the less collectable it is; and (2) if we finance customer purchases we are in effect lending them money we could be using for a better purpose.

PROFITABILITY RATIOS

Profitability ratios usually compare profit to sales, assets, or owners' equity. These ratios express the rate of return on money and labor committed in a business enterprise.

Rate of Return on Assets. This ratio tells how many cents of profit are generated for every dollar of assets the company owns. If the net profit of the company is $10,000, and the total assets are $100,000, the rate of return on assets is 10 percent. The derivation:

$$\text{Rate of Return on Assets}$$
$$= \frac{\text{Net Income}}{\text{Total Assets}}$$
$$= \frac{\$10,000}{\$100,000}$$
$$= 10\%$$

All assets should help make the company profitable, and selective use of this ratio can give us such information about all or most of the company's assets.

Rate of Return on Sales. This ratio tells how much profit is made for every dollar of sales. The formula is:

$$\text{Rate of Return on Sales} = \frac{\text{Net Income}}{\text{Sales}}$$

Assuming a net income of $10,000 and sales of $200,000, the Rate of Return on Sales is 5 percent ($10,000/$200,000). For every $1 in sales the profit was $.05.

Rate of Return on Owners' Equity. This ratio indicates profit in terms of owners' share of the assets. It is derived thus:

$$\text{Rate of Return on Owners' Equity}$$
$$= \frac{\text{Net Income}}{\text{Owners' Equity}}$$

If the net income is $10,000 and owners' equity is $50,000, the rate of return on owners' equity is 20 percent ($10,000/$50,000).

In our examples the profitability ratios have shown that for every $1 of sales the profit was $.05 (*rate of return on sales*); for every $1 of things the company owned the profit was $.10 (*rate of return on assets*); and for every dollar the owners had in the company the profit was $.20 (*rate of return on owners' equity*).

SUMMARY

In this chapter we have seen how the financial statements, taken together, can give the manager valuable information for making business decisions. Specifically we have examined the variety of facts that can be derived from the balance sheet and the income & expense statement, with their supporting schedules.

Using ratios, in some cases expressed as percentages, we have discovered what typical situation might obtain in a company with respect to:

a.   How much money it has on hand to meet its debts (*liquidity*).

b. How much business activity its money is producing (*working capital ratio*).

c. How much business is being generated with others' money (*leverage*).

d. How fast it sells its products (*inventory turnover*).

e. How quick its customers pay up (*accounts receivable turnover*).

f. How much the company earns per sale, how much its owners earn, and how much all its assets earn (*profitability ratios*)

These examples show some of the fruits to be harvested from a careful analysis of financial statements, and should whet our appetites for more.

STUDY QUESTIONS

1. If *liquidity* tells generally how fluid our assets are, what does *solvency* say further about our company's financial position?

2. State the formula for the *quick ratio*. How does it differ from the *current ratio* formula?

3. Figuring *leverage* on the basis of the ratio of total debts to total assets, would you consider 80 percent debt financing to be excessive? Discuss briefly.

4. Give two good reasons for using other people's money in business operations.

5. Name two *activity ratios* and explain their use.

6. How is the *accounts receivable turnover* used to compute the number of days it takes to collect from the average customer?

7. What is the formula for computing the *rate of return on assets?*

8. With reference to question 7 above, name two other *profitability ratios*.

CHAPTER **6**

COMPARISONS: INSIDE AND OUT

Universal bench marks for sizing up a business

PURPOSE

To investigate ways and means of measuring the success of business operations through internal and external analysis; in particular, to examine the
uniform accounting system adopted in the foodservice industry and see how
it serves management in comparing current and previous operating periods
and in matching them against industry averages.

CONTENT

The Comparative Analysis Process

The *Uniform System of Accounts for Restaurants*

Internal Analysis
  Balance sheet comparisons
  Income & expense comparisons
  Internal trends

The "Mean" and "Median" in Business Statistics

External Analysis
  Scouting the competition
  Industry-wide trends

Use of the Common Statement in Business Comparisons

MAKING COMPARISONS is a common practice in our daily lives. Almost without thinking we compare one thing with another dozens, if not hundreds, of times a day. For example, when a motorist remarks that his automobile is not getting as much mileage to a gallon of gas as it should, he is comparing the performance of his car to that of a similar make or model of automobile. He is comparing the performance of his car to what he regards as a standard. The motorist may use the information provided by the comparison to determine a course of action, such as to have the car serviced. Or, further consideration may indicate that servicing the automobile would not sufficiently improve his mileage to warrant the expense. So he decides to keep the car for another year and then buy a new one.

Recognizing how important the comparative process can be in decision-making, managers of business enterprises long ago began refining the process and have developed an elaborate system for exploiting it. This formalized system is generally referred to as comparative analysis. In analyzing their operations, managers study their organization internally and externally. They compare this year's operations with those of prior years and relate them all to plans for the future. Then they may extend their analysis to studies of similar operations, and to statistics on the entire industry. In making these studies they are likely to use, in addition to data generated on foodservice operations, a variety of social and economic indices bearing on the problem locally, regionally, and nationally.

UNIFORM RESTAURANT ACCOUNTING

In recognition of the growing demand of the industry for authentic operating data and financial guidance, the National Restaurant Association appointed, in 1967, a cost study committee. This committee concluded that a necessary step would be to renew interest in the *Uniform System of Accounts for Restaurants*. The principal objectives of the Uniform System are: (1) To provide restaurant operators with a common language for analyzing their financial operations; and (2) To promote a widespread development of data and statistical studies on the restaurant industry based on uniform accounting methods—all to the purpose of guiding the restaurateur to successful operations.

Previous work on this subject was expanded, and statement presentation and terminology were modernized in accordance with the latest business and accounting trends so a uniform arrangement would be arrived at that could be used by restaurants, regardless of type or size. The use of this system of accounting has not only made possible broad industry comparisons, but has allowed foodservice organizations to be categorized into various types for more detailed study.

Perhaps it should be noted here that any system of accounting which satisfies owners and the various government agencies might be called a "good" system; however, it may not be adequate for meaningful comparisons either internally or externally. To satisfy this requirement foodservice organizations need a common system. For example: Two foodservice companies, A and B, both show on their income & expense statement an account titled Administrative and General Expense. Company A includes in this expense item all advertising and promotion expense. Company B carries advertising and promotion expense as a separate item on its income & expense statement. Both statements might well be adequate for internal purposes, but their A&G expense accounts clearly would not be comparable.

INTERNAL COMPARISONS

Using both the income & expense statement and the balance sheet in the analysis of a business, one way to evaluate performance is to compare the operations and financial position of the company this year against those of prior years. This is not a foolproof method of analysis, but does definitely indicate areas that management should give attention to.

To show that both statements can and should be used in internal comparative analysis, Exhibits 6–1 and 6–2 will be used as examples. Year 3 will be considered the latest year of operation. On this basis the following might be observed in looking at the balance sheet in Exhibit 6–1 (see p. 68).

Starting with years 1 and 2, we find that the account called chattel mortgages due shows a sizable change, from $11,750 to $146,657, a total increase of $134,907. It appears that this capital was used for a new construction, since the property, plant & equipment account changed during the same period from $113,178 to $306,277, an increase of $193,099. To explain the difference between the increases in the plant & equipment and the chattel mortgage accounts we look to two other accounts, retained earnings and due to stockholders. Apparently money was borrowed from stockholders to help meet accounts payable as, again, our inspection shows a decided drop in this account.

A look at year 1 shows that it was necessary to borrow money and leave any retained earnings to finance the business. This we can tell because, although the current ratio is only slightly below 1:1 (current assets of $94,683 to current liabilities of $108,223), we have only $30,718 in cash to pay off current obligations of $94,303 (a 1:3 ratio). If all creditors had demanded immediate payment of their bills there would not have been enough cash. In a tight-money market the corporation would face serious liquidity problems.

Looking now at year 2 and year 3 on the balance sheet of Exhibit 6–1, we note that the cash and securities account has increased considerably. Two other accounts could easily explain this increase: accounts payable has increased, which indicates that the foodservice has not paid all of its current obligations, and earnings have again been left in the corporation as indicated by an increase in the retained earnings account.

The ability of the corporation to meet its current obligations has improved over the three years. In year 1 the current ratio was less than 1:1, while

ABC Corporation
BALANCE SHEET
For Years 19xx, 19xx and 19xx

	Year 3	Year 2	Year 1
Current Assets			
Cash and Securities	$116,273	$ 26,442	$ 30,718
Accounts Receivable (Less Allow.)	3,164	6,890	7,594
Inventories	23,297	24,169	15,400
Prepaid Expenses	27,279	17,530	40,971
Total Current Assets	$170,013	$ 75,031	$ 94,683
Due from Stockholders	—	—	7,087
Property, Plant & Equipment (Less Depr.)	304,108	306,277	113,178
Goodwill	18,578	18,578	18,578
TOTALS	$492,699	$399,886	$233,521
Current Liabilities			
Accounts Payable	$ 93,857	$ 32,430	$ 94,303
Accrued Taxes	12,103	18,605	11,538
Accrued Wages, Interest	2,950	2,438	2,382
Total Current Liabilities	$108,910	$ 53,472	$108,223
Due to Stockholders	34,648	42,495	—
Chattel Mortgages Due	148,237	146,657	11,750
Other Mortgages Due	10,000	10,000	10,000
Stockholders' Equity			
Common Stock—1,000 shares authorized, 4,270 Outstanding	42,740	41,740	41,740
Retained Earnings	148,164	105,521	61,808
TOTALS	$492,699	$399,886	$233,521

EXHIBIT 6–1   A report comparing the current balance sheet with data for previous years.

in years 2 and 3 it has improved to approximately 1.5:1. The relationship of the cash and securities account to accounts payable has improved even more dramatically. The ratio of these accounts has moved from a 1:3 in year 1 to approximately 1:1 in year 2 and 1.5:1 in year 3. This would indicate that the company was improving its cash position each year.

EXTERNAL COMPARISONS

Since management is directly accountable for sales and expense, its primary concern may well be with the income & expense statement, which indicates how successful it has been in operating the company (Exhibit 6–2). It will therefore be interested in comparing the income statement with prior years, with statements from similar companies, and with figures showing industry averages. For ease in analysis all such figures are stated as percentages. Total sales, or revenue, is always established as 100 percent, and expense is shown as a percentage of that figure. The percentage figure for any expense item indicates its relation to sales.

Exhibit 6–2 provides an example of an income & expense statement prepared for the purpose of making comparisons with national averages. Year 3 (from the balance sheet, Exhibit 6–1) is used in this example. The sales and expense figures have been converted to percentages. The national averages used are as published in an appendix of the *Uniform System of Accounts for Restaurants* for operations such as that of the ABC Corporation.

Referring to Exhibit 6–2, we note

the following: While expense percentages for year 3 conform fairly closely to the national average, there is one notable exception, in the classification administration and general expenses. The ABC Corporation has included in this classification an expense, officers salaries, which the national survey does not include. To make it comparable, excluding 9 percent (3/4 of the A&G expense) of the total controllable expense, the total for year 3 would in fact show a more profitable operating result than the national average.

By examining the variations between the ABC Corporation and the national average, management can readily pinpoint where it stands on expenses and costs. For example, the overall food cost in the ABC Corporation is 1.9 percent lower than the national figure based on actual restaurant operations. Even though individual variances may appear to be small, in the aggregate they can represent important differences in the corporation's bank account.

Looking now at Exhibit 6–3, which compares year 3 and year 2, we see that although total sales for year 3 have increased over sales for year 2, the cost of sales figure (food purchased) has also increased, thereby decreasing the total income. Comparing this year's performance to last year's may not be valid in all cases, but usually it is a good point to start the analysis. Even though internal comparisons may show steady improvement, management should be cautious in drawing conclusions if, in comparison with the national average, it falls short of its goals. *And,* even if it is exceeding the results shown by like organizations

ABC Corporation
INCOME & EXPENSE STATEMENT
Year Ending Dec. 31, 19xx

	Year 3		National Averages 1969
	Amount	*Percent*	
TOTAL SALES	$1,605,995	100.0%	100.0%
Cost of Sales			
Food (after credit for employee meals)	555,402	34.6	36.5
Gross Profit	$1,050,593	65.4	63.5
Other Income			.4
Total Income	$1,050,593	65.4	63.9
Controllable Expenses			
Payroll	477,284	29.7	33.1
Employee benefits	39,667	2.5	4.5
Direct operating expenses	73,849	4.6	5.4
Music and entertainment	—		
Advertising and promotion	911	.1	1.9
Utilities	30,374	1.9	1.9
Administrative and general	192,630	12.0	4.5
Repairs and maintenance	24,486	1.5	1.5
Total Controllable Expenses	$ 839,201	52.3	52.8
Income before Rent or Occupation Costs	211,392	13.1	11.1
Occupation Costs			
Rent or occupation costs	140,723	8.7	4.6
Depreciation	46,628	2.9	2.5
Income Tax	11,794	.7	
Total Occupation Costs	$ 199,145	12.3	7.1
NET PROFIT	$ 12,247	0.8%	4.0%

EXHIBIT 6–2   An income statement comparing current data with national averages, using percentages.

ABC Corporation
INCOME & EXPENSE STATEMENT

	Year 3		National Averages 1969	Year 2	
	Amount	Percent		Amount	Percent
TOTAL SALES	$1,605,995	100.0%	100.0%	$1,556,395	100.0%
Cost of Sales					
Food (after credit for employee meals)	555,402	34.6	36.5	527,005	33.9
Gross Profit	1,050,593	65.4	63.5	1,029,390	66.1
Other Income			.4		
Total Income	$1,050,593	65.4	63.9	1,029,390	66.1
Controllable Expenses					
Payroll	477,284	29.7	33.1	460,799	29.6
Employee benefits	39,667	2.5	4.5	38,110	2.5
Direct operating expenses	73,849	4.6	5.4	75,847	4.9
Music and entertainment	—			—	
Advertising and promotion	911	.1	1.9	973	.1
Utilities	30,374	1.9	1.9	26,584	1.7
Administrative and general	192,630	12.0	4.5	192,389	12.4
Repairs and maintenance	24,486.	1.5	1.5	23,629	1.5
Total Controllable Expenses	$ 839,201	52.3	52.8	$ 818,331	52.7
Income before Rent or Occupation Costs	211,392	13.1	11.1	211,059	13.4
Occupation Costs					
Rent or occupation costs	140,723	8.7	4.6	132,234	8.4
Depreciation	46,628	2.9	2.5	45,152	2.9
Income Tax	11,794	.7		16,604	1.0
Total Occupation Costs	$ 199,145	12.3	7.1	$ 193,990	12.3
NET PROFIT	$ 12,247	0.8%	4.0%	$ 17,069	1.1%

EXHIBIT 6–3 Last two income statements compared to national averages.

in the national averages, management should recognize that its organization may be one of those in the position of *improving* the national averages.

Management decisions are often influenced by trends. In taking note of trends it is important to be aware that, generally speaking, a change that runs for less than three years does not constitute a valid trend. Sometimes it takes five or even ten years to establish a reliable business trend.

Mean and Median

Two words often used by management when discussing the operations of a company are *mean* and *median*. These words look and sound alike and they are sometimes confused, but they are *not* the same. *The mean is an average of a list of numbers,* the mathematical mean. *The median is the middle number in a series,* with half the numbers above and half below that number. To illustrate: A foodservice operator wishes to find the mean and median points in a series of guest checks to help in making a pricing decision. Nine checks are chosen at random from the number turned in by the waitress that day. The following checks are listed:

Check number	Amount
1	$10.00
2	9.00
3	5.00
4	4.00
5	3.00 = Median
6	2.50
7	2.50
8	1.00
9	1.00

$$\$38.00 \div 9 = 4.22 \text{ (Mean)}$$

To find the mean (or average), the total amount of the nine checks would be divided by the number of checks ($38 divided by 9) and an average check value of $4.22 would be determined.

In finding the median, the number would be chosen that was the middle number, in this case check number 5. Check number 5 would have four checks with a greater amount above it and four checks with a smaller amount below it. In this example the median would be $3.

In the above example the median and mean have come fairly close. Let's take another example to illustrate a more drastic difference, choosing five checks as follows:

Check number	Amount
1	$15
2	14
3	12 = Median
4	3
5	2

$$\$46 \div 5 = \$9.20 \text{ (Mean)}$$

In the second example, the mean—found by dividing the total amount of the items by the number of items—would be $9.20. The median, picking the middle number—the one with two values above it and two below it—would be $12.

Scouting the Competition

To keep up with the competition many business houses employ "shoppers"—persons who make purchases in competitors' establishments to compare price, value, service, and so on. Some foodservice operators often dine in competing establishments to observe their prices, food, service, decor, cleanliness and other points of interest. Managers of large companies have been known to buy stock in competitive firms in order to receive regular financial reports from these companies for comparative analysis. Most foodservice operators find it highly advantageous to keep abreast of what their competitors are doing, as an aid in evaluating their own policies and practices.

The operator must, however, be judicious in reaching conclusions from external comparisons, because seldom is the whole picture presented. The business in a neighborhood restaurant will vary from that in a downtown location or one on a highway. To help the operator in his search for valid information, some accounting firms specialize in the hospitality industry. They prepare annual reports presenting statistics for the various categories of foodservice establishments. Statistical information is also available from time to time through the National Restaurant Association and other trade associations related to the hospitality industry, as well as through various government agencies and trade publications.

General information on the industry must be treated more cautiously than the information dealing with specific types of foodservice operations. The foodservice business may, in general, be showing a definite upward trend in sales; however, because of local conditions, the foodservice business in a particular community could be in a serious slump.

External trends affect a foodservice in different ways. As previously noted, these trends usually develop over a period of years. We find trends in the movement of people—from the city to the country, from one region to another, from houses to apartments. The alert manager will be aware of these trends by keeping comparative figures on his own operation and by watching developments in the industry. A number of years ago the trend was for customers to leave the coffee shop to eat in their automobile, and the drive-in developed. In recent years this trend has leveled off. Once again people seem to prefer to eat inside.

The Common Statement

In addition to the Uniform System of Accounts, restaurant operators also use the *common statement* to facilitate comparative analysis. The common statement shows sales, controllable expenses, rent, occupancy cost, and other accounts as percentages, using sales as 100 percent (see Exhibit 6–4). The common statement enables management to make comparisons with similar operations, regardless of size. If Store A sells $100,000 a year, and Store B has sales of $165,000, their operations are more readily compared when income and expense are stated as percentages of sales. Also, comparisons can be made without divulging actual sales or expense figures. Some companies would not let actual sales and expense figures be made public, but will release percentage figures as presented in common statements.

There are some limitations to the common statement. For example, a small foodservice proprietorship or partnership will typically show an owner withdrawal of funds as a distribution of profits rather

ABC Corporation
INCOME & EXPENSE STATEMENT
(Common)

	Year 1 Percentage
TOTAL SALES	100.0%
Cost of Sales	
Food (after credit for employee meals)	34.6
Gross Profit	65.4
Other Income	0
Total Income	65.4
Controllable Expenses	
Payroll	29.7
Employee benefits	2.5
Direct operating expenses	4.6
Music and entertainment	0
Advertising and promotion	.1
Utilities	1.9
Administrative and general	12.0
Repairs and maintenance	1.5
Total Controllable Expenses	52.3
Income before Rent or Occupation Costs	13.1
Occupation Costs	
Rent or occupation costs	8.7
Depreciation	2.9
Income Tax	.7
Total Occupation Costs	12.3
NET PROFIT	0.8%

EXHIBIT 6–4 The common statement, using percentages for easy comparison.

than an expense of the business. If the same operation had been a corporation, the amount withdrawn would be included as an expense item on the income statement. For the most part these transactions are handled differently because of income tax requirements.

An inherent limitation of the common statement hinges on the fact that small operations are not in all respects comparable to large operations. A large enterprise will usually have a substantial amount of administrative expense, advertising, and a sophisticated accounting system, while in the small operation these costs will be relatively much smaller. Nevertheless, it can be seen that the common statement is a valuable instrument in comparative studies.

The assumptions under which the accountant works impose other limits on the usefulness of financial statements in making comparisons. Plant assets, for example, are recorded at cost, and if the asset is depreciable the accountant depreciates the cost rather than the fair market value or replacement cost. Suppose that some years ago Company A acquired a kitchen which cost $50,000 to furnish, and that this kitchen will last 10 years. Depreciation on a straight-line basis would be $5,000 a year for 10 years.

Company B, which has just opened, has acquired the same kitchen equipment but at a cost of $100,000. Company B will have depreciation expense of $10,000 per year for 10 years. From this it can be seen that Company A and Company B have identical kitchens, but Company A will show on its income statement a depreciation expense of only $5,000 while Company B will show a depreciation expense of $10,000.

SUMMARY

The ordinary process of making decisions by comparisons has been systematized in the business world. Foodservice managers use comparative analysis in a variety of ways to help reach a better understanding of their business operations and to improve their decision-making capability.

To provide foodservice operators with authentic data on operating results, and guidance in solving financial problems, the National Restaurant Association published the *Uniform System of Accounts for Restaurants*. This book gives restaurant operators a common accounting language enabling them to compare their operations with those of other companies, and promotes the development of valuable statistical data on an industry-wide basis.

The income & expense statement and the balance sheet are used in both the internal and external analysis of business operations. The income & expense statement is of primary interest in studying sales and expense since it deals with the operations of the company.

Significant trends usually cover a period of three years or more. Management should consider trends for their effect on future business as well as for their immediate effect. Political, social and economic developments may seriously affect both sales and expense of the foodservice operation and should be a part of any comparative study.

The *common statement* shows costs and expenses as percentages of sales. It allows a company to report on its operations without divulging actual sales or cost figures. The common statement enables the management of any business to compare its operations with those of any other regardless of size.

Fundamental differences between reporting companies limit the usefulness of comparative analyses based on financial statements alone, but most foodservice companies find this process of considerable value in planning and evaluating their operations.

STUDY QUESTIONS

1. Why was the *Uniform System of Accounts for Restaurants* developed? Aside from its significance for the accounting process, how does it serve management?

2. Describe the type of information a foodservice manager might look for in comparing his balance sheets with industry averages.

3. Why is a foodservice manager especially interested in the income & expense statement when analyzing operations?

4. Explain why the foodservice manager is interested in industry trends.

5. Discuss briefly the minimum time base required for a statistically valid trend.

6. What is the outstanding feature of the common statement used in comparative studies? Identify two limiting features of this statement.

7. Illustrate in a simple example the difference between a *mean* and a *median* in a series of numbers.

8. What general caution should an operator observe in external analysis based on visits to competitors' restaurants?

PART THREE

HOW THE MANAGER
USES ACCOUNTING DATA

CHAPTER 7

THE COST OF DOING BUSINESS

If it cost too much we couldn't be doing it

PURPOSE

To explore the significance of cost in business operations, with a view to discovering how the accounting system deals with it, and how a typical foodservice manager uses accounting data in controlling costs and optimizing profits.

CONTENT

Cost and Expense: The Accounting Technique
    Costs as assets
    Types of cost defined

Cost Accounting and Management

Costs and Profit Planning

A Practical Foodservice Case
    Occupation costs
    Operating costs

Cost Control: A Preview

COST & EXPENSE: THE ACCOUNTING TECHNIQUE

FOR THE ACCOUNTANT, COSTS ARE ASSETS. On the face of it that is a shocker for the businessman, or any of us who think of cost as an outlay of work or treasure—a minus, not a plus—to obtain something we want. And an asset *is* a plus, isn't it?

This is a subject worth conjuring with, and elsewhere we examine the terminology of cost accounting, but don't take it purely on faith that a cost is an asset. There is a real lesson for the business manager in this accounting concept. The accountant is not just playing games of double entry when he puts costs under assets on the left side of the big T ledger. He is telling us that if we have no goods or services to sell, there can be no sale, that without input there is no output. He is saying, in essence, that it takes value to produce value.

"Double entry"? How long did it take you to do a *double take* on that? The accountant, we said, registers costs on the left as assets. What does he do on the right? He doesn't—not yet. And thereby hangs a very important point. Nothing happens on the right side of our equation until something happens with those assets on the left. So where is the double entry? The answer is that the accountant keeps the equation in balance by making *two* equal and opposite entries on the left side! In purchasing inventory for cash, for example, he trades one asset for another. But that does not explain the big point, which is that assets remain assets until they are expended, and then they become *expenses*.

As we note in the boxed insert, expenses are described as expired or "gone" assets. Not until an asset (cost) is used up in generating revenue does the accountant move it to the "operating" side of the equation, where it is treated as a plus under revenue and a minus under expense. Both revenue and expense, you will recall, are tributaries to capital (owner's equity), otherwise known as net assets. If this sounds like double talk or even triple talk, don't be dismayed. What you call it depends fundamentally upon whether you are looking at the matter from the standpoint of the company— the assets view—or from the standpoint of the contributor of assets—the equity view. In either case the accountant's overall view of the matter satisfies the general equation $A = L + C$. When assets expire, are consumed, given up, used— however you wish to put it—the record accounts for them equally, on both sides of the equation. Assets are credited, and capital is debited. And equilibrium is maintained. Both sides of the big T account remain in balance.

We mentioned triple talk. Accountants seem to have more than one way to look at almost every element in their reckoning. No doubt this is inherent in the art, since there are so many ways to analyze business transactions—from the viewpoint of the investor of funds and from that of the user of funds, to say nothing of the special case in which both of these come together in the owner-operator. But three is not an even number, and to speak of triple talk is unrealistic. We could hardly come out even with triple entries, and no one is suggesting that we could. *Quadruple* entries are, however, not unrealistic at all. That

---

TERMINOLOGY

"My costs are no problem. It's the expenses I dread." The manager who can say this with conviction, and who understands what he or she is saying, has come pretty far in comprehending business theory.

Costs represent *goods,* or the right to use something tangible like buildings and machinery, and even intangibles like labor, in turning out products and services. The problem is to some extent a matter of words and the special meanings they are given in technical usage. But it is helpful to rationalize the technical use of a word, if only to make it easier to remember its special meaning. In wrestling with the terms *cost* and *expense,* try this: What comes to mind when someone talks about "how much it cost"? Think about it. If *it* is a thing of lasting value, the idea of worth is there—what it can do for you. When we talk about a service or a thing we buy and use up right away, we may mention how much we "paid" for it, but we are not so inclined to speak of its "cost." That, in any case, is pretty close to how the manufacturer or tradesman should distinguish between cost and expense.

In accounting, a *cost* is defined as an asset. The term is often applied to what we pay for goods or services, but *cost* should not be treated as a synonym for *expense.* An expense is a kind of cost—an "expired" cost, but all costs are not expenses—yet. The accountant defines *expense* as the cost of assets expended in generating revenue.

Here are some other definitions which relate to the material in the present chapter:

Product costs—The costs associated directly with the production of a commodity, such as the raw materials cost, labor cost, fuel cost, and the like.

Period costs—The costs incurred in managing, maintaining and developing the business, such as rent, insurance, taxes, and other expenses not linked directly to a product and which would occur even if there were no production.

Prime cost—Total cost of materials and labor assigned directly to a product. In most foodservice operations prime cost represents approximately 70 percent of sales revenue.

is precisely what we do have when we go full-tilt into the accounting experience and deal with the sale of an asset. On the *asset* side we debit cash (an increase) and credit inventory (a decrease), and on the *capital* side we debit expense (an increase on the minus side) and credit revenue (an increase on the plus side). And all comes out in the wash on our balance sheet.[1]

Our account is indeed in balance after all these entries, but a further point needs to be made with respect to how assets are converted. There are in general two kinds of conversion. The cost of fixed assets such as plant and equipment is converted to expense over a long period in accordance with a predetermined schedule of depreciation. The cost of inventory is converted and expensed as the goods are sold in creating revenue. The latter may occur very rapidly in a food-service with its quick turnover of stock, especially in the case of perishable fresh produce.

Any expense is at least technically a cost, and subject to the same kind of analysis in cost control; but some expenses never see the light of day as costs in the strict accounting sense because of

---

1. If you go back to Event VI in the transaction analysis of Chapter 2, you will note that we deliberately used some shorthand in illustrating a point. Now that score is even: When the restaurant sold $500 worth of food we added it to cash under *A* and likewise added it to revenue under *C*. But now we know that when cost and expense are considered we also have to subtract from *A* by decreasing inventory and subtract from *C* by increasing expense. Refer also to Exhibit 2–5 for an all-in-one picture of which accounts are debited and which are credited on the Big T of accounting.

their intangible nature or because they are too short-lived ever to be carried on the books as assets. In this category are advertising costs and other outlays necessary in earning income (the cost of selling), also wages and administrative costs, including the cost of clerical supplies— pencils and paper, for instance, which would hardly be taken up as inventory except in the event of liquidating the business at a time when they existed in considerable quantity. These are all a very real part of business costs, but by the time they are recognized in the accounting process they have already become expired costs and are therefore registered as expenses.

Labor clearly represents a major cost item in business operations but, because it is not a physical commodity we can see, measure and store, it is not treated as an asset. On the other hand prepaid expenses, like funds reserved for payment of future obligations, can be so measured and held and, like cash, are carried on the books as assets.

Without exploring the history of accounting techniques more than our present survey would justify, we can only speculate that the wizards who originated double-entry bookkeeping had these problems in mind when they classified expenses, like other costs, as debit accounts that have the same effect as assets in the balancing out of debits and credits.

COST ACCOUNTING AND MANAGEMENT

So much for the mechanics of accounting for costs and their sidekick, expenses. Granting the ingenuity involved in developing the system originally, we might be inclined to dismiss the data-gathering and entry-making as cut-and-dried bookkeeping procedures. But identifying expenses and matching them up with the revenues they were instrumental in producing is quite another matter. Here the accountant really hits his professional stride, and his services to management become most significant.

Although some would extend their role, accountants are not by nature entrepreneurs. They are not, as accountants, responsible for acquiring assets, whether by increases in creditor investment (liabilities) or owner investment (capital). That is the province of the business managers. Nor does the accountant participate directly in decisions calculated to increase capital (net assets) through additions to income (sales revenue). Even as the comptroller or chief accounting officer of a corporation, the accountant leaves these decisions to other members of the executive team.

In dealing with costs, however, the accountant comes into his own. He is no longer playing a passive role or merely reacting to facts in the accounting record. In computing and allocating costs he is exercising judgment in his special sphere of competence. We may say that cost accounting, an elaborate specialty in itself —and of critical importance in many manufacturing operations—is the very heart of the accounting problem, especially as it relates to the all-essential function of measuring earnings.

COSTS AND PROFIT PLANNING

We have previously indicated that managers instinctively characterize cost as an outlay for the purpose of achieving a desired result. And we have seen that they had to take a technical turn or two to reconcile their view with that of the accountant. Let us now see if it is not a very simple matter to identify the manager's purpose as that of optimizing profits: obtaining the best possible return on the company's investment. We say it is the optimum rather than the maximum that he seeks because, for one thing, there is a limit to the volume of sales a given enterprise can accommodate, and, for another, the operator may have definite ideas about the desirable size of the enterprise. Also, the operator may well have other than commercial objectives in operating a business.

How, then, does the business manager optimize costs and sales in a manner consistent with the particular profit-planning goals of the operation? Let's examine this question from the position of a typical foodservice operator, emphasizing the element of costs.

A PRACTICAL CASE

Profit planning rests heavily on the identification of two types of costs—*fixed cost* and *variable cost*. Fixed costs are those that remain constant irrespective of the volume of sales. Variable costs change with sales volume—the greater the number of persons served and the number of meals produced, the greater the variable cost.

Occupation Costs—Open or Not

We will assume that our foodservice operator is already in business and owns the restaurant and the land on which it sits. If the operator chooses to shut down and take an extended vacation, does he have any continuing expense on his property? The answer is definitely yes. The following would have to be paid:

Insurance—Even if the establishment is closed and boarded up, the property must be covered for possible damage by fire, windstorm, vandalism, etc.

Property tax—This tax is operable whether the restaurant is open or closed.

Notes Payable—If there is a mortgage loan or other debt outstanding, the lender will expect interest payments (and usually principal payments) to be made regardless of whether the restaurant is open for business.

Depreciation—Whether the building, equipment and furniture are in use or not, these assets depreciate in value simply with the passage of time.

The above expenses are not necessarily the only ones a propertyowner has. A local sewer tax or a personal property tax might also have to be paid. All such expenses represent the cost of ownership, and they continue in effect whether the business is in operation or not. For purposes of this discussion we will consider these as *occupation expenses.*

Operating Costs

We may now ask what additional expenses are incurred when the restaurant *is* open for business. It must have a basic staff on the job whether it serves one customer or a hundred. In a medium-size

restaurant this basic staff might consist of a cook and one or more helpers, a hostess, cashier, steward, assistant manager, and a minimum number of service personnel, representing the costs of payroll, payroll taxes and benefits, and perhaps employee meals and uniforms.

Further, there will be some utilities costs for gas, electricity, water and telephone. Any advertising or other sales promotion expense must also be included in the cost of being open for business, as well as the costs of maintenance and repairs, licenses, etc., regardless of the customer load. These additional expenses that the operator incurs as the result of the decision to be open we will designate as *primary expenses.*

Once the operator has occupied the premises and decided to open the door, does it make any difference, in terms of additional cost, how many customers are served? As we can readily see, the answer again is yes. For reliable cost analysis it is therefore necessary to keep accurate sales records. Depending upon the type of operation, this can be done by means of a cashier count, a "covers" count kept by the kitchen, or a record compiled from the "number of persons served" entered on the guest check. One way or other a cumulative record of the number of customers served should be maintained throughout the year.

What additional expenses can the operator expect as a result of serving many customers instead of a few? Here are some:

Laundry—The more times table linen is changed the greater the laundering costs will be, and increased demand on the supply of fresh uniforms may also be a factor.

Paper supplies—The use of guest checks, paper napkins, "daily receipts and expense" report forms, etc., will increase with additional sales.

Part-time payroll—The cost of additional kitchen, dining room and supervisory personnel will likewise be directly affected by increased customer traffic.

Tableware replacement—With more frequent usage, chinaware, glassware and silverware will more often be damaged or lost and have to be replaced.

These are examples of expenses we may call *serving expenses*. They represent the direct cost of serving guests and will increase as the number of guests increases. With accurate data these expenses can easily be calculated on a dollar-and-cents basis per customer, as follows: Assume that last year the restaurant served a total of 200,000 customers. If $6,000 was spent replacing tableware, this means that on the average it cost $.03 (200,000 into $6,000) to serve each customer. If you had only 100,000 customers and the breakage and loss were the same, your replacement expense per customer would be $.06.

Last but certainly not least we come to the cost represented by the product itself, the food and beverages served to the customer. When the customer orders a steak dinner, for example, does it cost anything additional to serve him that dinner over and above *occupation expenses, primary expenses* and *serving ex-*

penses? Assuredly it does, and this is what we refer to as *product cost,* or, more commonly, the *cost of goods sold*. This cost is the raw cost to the operator of providing food to patrons. Patrons, of course, must pay him an amount greater than the cost of food, since he has to meet all his other expenses and still make a profit.

We can now place our four types of cost into two categories: *Occupation expenses* and *primary expenses* are classified as FIXED COSTS, and *serving expenses* and *cost of goods sold* are classified as VARIABLE COSTS. And we have come full circle, back to our original definitions.

Before we leave our brief analysis of costs in foodservice profit planning it may be useful to mention another group of costs which have both fixed and variable components. Such costs are known as *semivariable costs* and are of practical significance to the restaurant operator. Utilities are an example. There is a basic standard cost of service (the fixed component) which increases with usage but on a descending scale of cost per unit (the variable component). Charges for electric power, for example, are based on a fixed charge plus a charge for each kilowatt-hour over and above the standard usage. Further, the rate per kilowatt-hour decreases with additional usage, so that while the absolute dollar expense increases as more electricity is used, the unit cost is less.

COST CONTROL: A PREVIEW

Costs, fixed and variable, constitute only one of the two major elements in profit planning, and do not tell the complete story except when analyzed in conjunction with sales. This we will see done in the following chapter on break-even analysis.

From our foregoing discussions it is clear that systematic efforts to identify and account for costs are of first importance to success in business operations. Indeed, that is the "financial ingredient" to which we refer in the title of this book and which, space permitting, we might have called an indispensable ingredient. But what the business manager ultimately wants is to *control* his costs. This subject is grist enough for a shelfful of books but some aspects of the problem are covered in the final chapters of the present volume, which focus on the major targets of cost control—food costs and labor costs.

SUMMARY

The seeming paradox that costs are accounted for as assets is dispelled when we appreciate that it takes value to produce value, and that a reasonable return on materials and labor invested in business transactions normally represents a small proportion of the total values exchanged.

The accountant construes cost as an asset so long as the item—fixed assets or inventory—has the potential to produce revenue. He "expenses" the item when it no longer has this potential—as, for example, when machinery wears out or when goods in inventory are sold.

In accounting for costs—charging them against the *product* which required them, or against the *period* in which they were incurred—the accountant is performing a most significant service to management: the important first step in controlling costs and measuring earnings.

The foodservice operator can very usefully analyze costs from the standpoint of fixed costs and variable costs. The first category includes *occupation costs,* which are present whether the restaurant is open or not, and *primary expenses* which represent minimum operational costs. The second category embraces costs that vary with the level of business activity: *serving expenses* and the *cost of goods sold.*

Cost control, the ultimate object of the operator in considering the "financial ingredient" in the management function, relies to a great extent on the information and guidance provided by the accounting system.

STUDY QUESTIONS

1. Define *cost* in the accounting sense.
2. Describe *expense* in terms of the general concept of cost.
3. Discuss in about 50 words your conception of cost accounting as an element in profit planning.
4. What are product costs? Contrast with period costs.

5. In our foodservice example, what are the two components of fixed costs?

6. What other major category of costs is composed of *serving expenses* and *cost of goods sold,* as presented in our example?

7. Give an example of a *semivariable cost,* and explain briefly.

8. What major element other than cost must be considered in determining profit?

CHAPTER 8

BREAK-EVEN ANALYSIS

A what-if *computer for almost every business problem*

Purpose

To demonstrate the use of break-even analysis, by graph and by mathematical formula, in determining how costs and profits vary as a function of sales; and to see how this information can be used in planning and controlling foodservice operations.

Content

The Function of Break-Even Analysis

Constructing the Break-Even Chart
    The vertical axis
    The horizontal axis
    Graphing sales
    Graphing fixed costs
    Graphing total costs
    Extracting the facts

The Break-Even Formula

Using the Break-Even Chart
    Spending the advertising dollar
    Competition: "Biting the bullet"
    Budgeting for profits
    Facing a rent hike

Reliability of Break-Even Projections

BOOST SALES. Cut costs. Increase profits. It seems that people in business are forever figuring ways to improve their operation. As indeed they must. But wouldn't it be better if they could do this by using a model instead of the costly trial-and-error method? It would and they can. It is like rearranging furniture: you don't have to move the piano to see if it will fit between the bookcase and the couch.

The model we have in mind is the familiar device that shows up in almost every book on business management—the break-even chart. This is not a magic wheel that you twirl for the magic answer. But, as with any calculator, if you have the inputs it has the answers.

The answers to what? Let's go back to big sales, low costs and high profits. Only one of these—high profits—is an absolute blessing under all conditions, and even that assumes you are in business purely for monetary gain. What break-even analysis does is to help us see the complex relationships that exist between a variety of factors in the business picture. And even when these answers are neatly displayed we have to do some careful picking-off of values and measuring between points and lines, if not curves.

The moral is that we will see better how the chart works and be able to use it more handily if we develop one ourselves. That's what we propose to do, and in doing so we will consider some typical *what-if?* questions facing a restaurant manager.

Spending the advertising dollar. "Right now," says Mrs. Jones, "I serve 40,000 meals a year. With some promotion and advertising, I could probably boost that figure to 50,000 meals. Of course, I don't want promotion and advertising costs to eat up all of the additional profits. How much would those additional profits amount to?"

"Biting the bullet" of competition. "With a franchise opening up across the street," says Mr. Smith, "I'm in a highly competitive situation. I may have to cut prices to stay in business. How much can I cut those prices?"

Budgeting for profits. "A local developer predicts a 20 percent increase in business next year," says Mrs. Brown, "Maybe it's not all blue-sky talk. If I were to share in this business increase, how should I budget my costs?"

Facing a rent hike. "My landlord wants to raise my rent 20 percent," says Mr. Johnson. "He just might do it. What increase in sales volume will I need to maintain my present profit level if I can't bargain him down?"

Each of these problems is different. Some of them assume increased business and others call for belt tightening. Even though each of the problems is different, the questions asked by these restaurant managers have a common theme. All of the questions deal with the way sales, costs and profits affect each other as these quantities change. Here, we are concerned about the *relationships* of changing quantities.

One of the best ways of representing

and understanding changing quantities is to graph them. And this is the purpose of the break-even chart. It is a graph that presents relationships between profits and costs at changing levels of sales volume.

Usually, a break-even chart is based on actual historical data. The graph projects this historical data and the projected data answers the kinds of questions asked by our imaginary restaurant managers.

CONSTRUCTING THE BREAK-EVEN CHART

In a step-by-step manner, we are going to build a break-even chart, explaining the inputs as we proceed. Then we will show how the chart answers questions about sales, costs and profit relationships. At the conclusion of this chapter, you will be able to construct and interpret a break-even chart based on your own operations.

Dollars on the vertical axis. To build our break-even chart (Exhibit 8–1), we need some basic information about past financial performance. One such item of information is total dollar sales for the past year. We'll assume this amounted to $200,000. Our chart should tell us about sales levels above and below the present level of $200,000. For example, we might want to know what would hap-

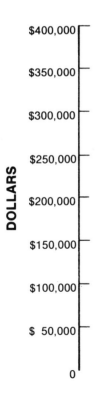

EXHIBIT 8–1   Vertical axis of the break-even chart.

pen to costs and profits if sales were to double. Our chart must cover a sales volume range of $400,000. Accordingly, this amount is laid out in $50,000 steps on the left-hand vertical axis of the chart. This is shown in Exhibit 8–1, where we have divided the vertical axis into steps up to the amount of the total sales volume in which we are interested.

Number of meals on the horizontal axis. Another item of basic historical information is the total number of meal checks for the same sales period. We'll assume total meal checks for the year amounted to 40,000. If total sales amounted to $200,000, and 40,000 meals were sold, then the amount of an average cover or meal check was $5.

As you recall, our break-even chart must show sales, costs and profit relationships up to $400,000 in sales. How many meals must we sell to reach this sales volume? At five dollars a meal, we must serve 80,000 meals to reach a sales volume of $400,000. Therefore, the horizontal (bottom) axis of the graph is laid off in 10,000-meal steps up to 80,000 meals. This is shown in Exhibit 8–2, where we

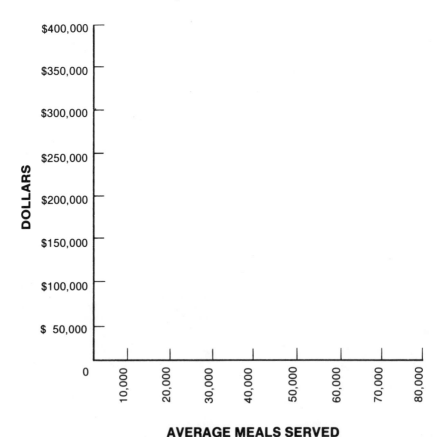

EXHIBIT 8–2   Vertical and horizontal axes.

have divided the horizontal axis into steps representing the number of average meals sold. The highest number of average meals sold will produce the maximum sales volume on the graph.

Graphing sales. Now we will graph total dollar sales by drawing a diagonal line from zero to the maximum projected sales volume, $400,000 in this case (see Exhibit 8–3).

Graphing fixed costs. The next step is to graph our costs. In preparing the break-even chart, it is important to distinguish between fixed costs and variable costs. This is true because these different types of costs affect profits in very different ways.

As the name suggests, fixed costs are relatively stable over the financial period being studied. These costs remain stable despite upward or downward changes in sales volume. Here are some examples of fixed costs:

Rent
Mortgage payments
Property taxes
Heating (noncooking)

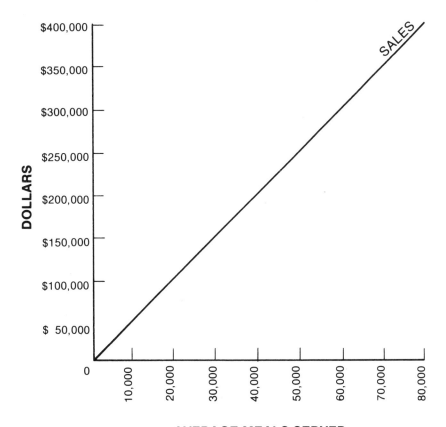

EXHIBIT 8–3   The sales line.

Electricity (noncooking)
Insurance
Depreciation
License fees

These costs will remain approximately constant even though there are changes in the number of guests or meals served.

For our example, we'll assume that fixed costs for the past year totaled $50,000. Since this amount is stable despite the number of meals served, we draw a straight line across the graph at the $50,000 level (see Exhibit 8–4).

Graphing total costs. In contrast to fixed costs, variable costs change with the dollar volume of sales. Variable costs increase as the number of meals served increases, and they decrease as the number of meals served decreases. Here are some examples of variable costs:

Food cost
Beverage cost

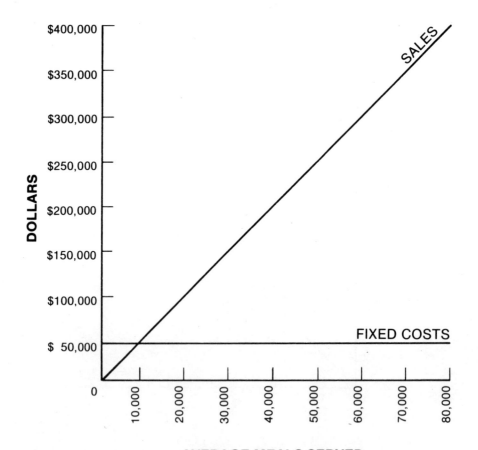

EXHIBIT 8–4   The fixed costs line.

Payroll and related expenses
Music and entertainment
Advertising and promotion
Direct operating expenses

In our example, the total of these variable costs amounted to $130,000 for the past year. During this same period, 40,000 meals were sold. It required $130,000 in variable costs to produce 40,000 meals.

To determine profits, we must subtract *total* costs from sales. Accordingly, we must graph *total* costs as well as fixed costs. Total costs are the sum of fixed and variable costs. With fixed costs of $50,000 and variable costs of $130,000, at a production volume of 40,000 meals our *total costs* amount to $180,000. As illustrated in Exhibit 8–5 this relationship is graphed by circling the intersection of 40,000 meals and $180,000.

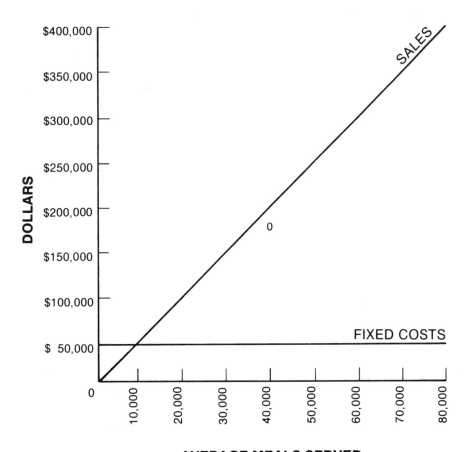

EXHIBIT 8–5 The intersection of meals served and total costs.

We have circled the intersection where the total number of meals served during the past year crosses the total cost level for the past year. This was done to help us graph the total cost line.

Our fixed costs are $50,000. If there were no variable costs, our total cost line should start at the $50,000 level. That same total cost line should intersect our $180,000 of total costs for the past year. We will graph this total cost line by connecting these two points and extending

the line to the edge of the graph, as shown in Exhibit 8–6.

We have graphed total costs by drawing a line between the point of zero variable costs (where fixed costs intersect the dollar axis) and the point representing total costs for the past year. Then, we extended this total cost line to the edge of the graph.

Extracting the facts. The graph now includes sales, total costs and fixed costs. We have also graphed variable costs in

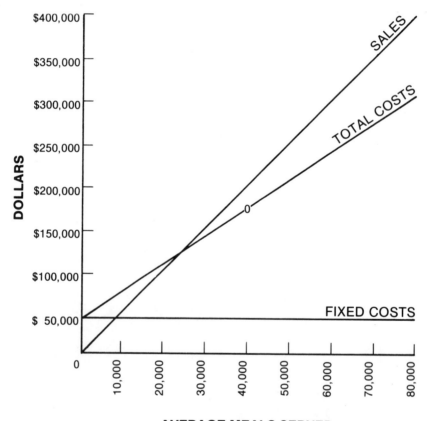

EXHIBIT 8–6   The total costs line.

the sense that variable costs are the difference between total costs and fixed costs. Income and expenses are also graphed in that they are the differences between total costs and sales.

We mentioned that a break-even chart was usually based on actual historical data. Let's see how well the chart represents these facts:

40,000 meals served
$ 50,000 fixed costs
$180,000 total costs
$200,000 total sales

By following up the vertical line at 40,000 meals on the chart in Exhibit 8–6, you will be able to confirm these data. Our chart does present the historical facts. Everything else on the chart is a projection based on these facts.

The break-even point. Notice the point in Exhibit 8–6 where the sales line crosses the total costs line. This is the break-even point. It tells us that, with our cost relationships, we will be losing money at all sales volumes below $140,000. Conversely, we should be making a profit at all sales volumes above $140,000.

THE BREAK-EVEN FORMULA

There is a simple equation that can be used in break-even analysis to determine the break-even point. The terms of this equation are as follows:

BEP = Break-even point in number of average meals sold
FC = Total fixed costs in dollars
SP = Selling price of an average meal
VC = Variable costs in dollars per average meal

The break-even equation is:

$$BEP = \frac{FC}{SP - VC}$$

We will use the break-even equation to confirm the break-even point shown in Exhibit 8–6.

$FC = \$50,000$
$SP = \$5.00$
$VC = \$3.25$

Substituting these data, the equation produces the following results:

$$BEP = \frac{\$50,000}{\$5 - 3.25}$$
$$BEP = \frac{\$50,000}{\$1.75}$$
$$BEP = 28,571$$

The calculated break-even point of 28,571 average meals served is close enough to confirm the break-even point of 30,000 average meals sold shown on the chart.

In constructing our break-even chart, we plotted the total-costs line by first locating the point where the number of average meals served intersects total costs. We did this by using historical data. The total-costs line can also be plotted by determining the break-even point by means of the break-even point equation, and then locating this point on the chart. A line connecting total fixed costs and the break-even point, extended to the edge of the chart, is the total-costs line.

USING THE BREAK-EVEN CHART

Remember the questions of those restaurant managers at the beginning of this chapter? Now we can answer those questions using projected data on the break-even chart in Exhibit 8–6. In all cases, we will assume that the restaurant manager is basing his questions on the same historical data that we have graphed.

Spending the advertising dollar. The first manager wanted to know how her profit picture would change if the number of meals served increased from 40,000 to 50,000. She could use this information to gauge expenditures for advertising and promotion.

From the chart in Exhibit 8–6, we can see that her before-tax profits amounted to approximately $20,000 last year. If meals served increases to 50,000, profits would increase to $40,000. This difference in profit levels of $20,000 would be partially consumed by advertising and other promotion costs. If the manager's assumption is correct—that by increasing advertising and promotion, the number of meals served will increase to 50,000—she would be wise to launch a promotion campaign offering reasonable hope of this $20,000 increase in profits.

"Biting the bullet" of competition. The second manager was bracing for a price war and wanted to know how far he could cut prices. If prices were cut to the extent of the $20,000 profit he is currently making, his average meal would drop from $5 to $4.50. Not very much. We don't need the break-even chart to determine this. However, our break-even chart gives us much more interesting and useful information about this problem.

Look at the break-even point on the chart in Exhibit 8–6. It shows that this manager could maintain present prices and still break even if the franchisee took away 12,000 meals, leaving his restaurant

only 28,000 meals to serve. In other words, this manager has a 12,000-meal cushion without cutting prices at all. He can afford to lose 30 percent (12,000/40,000) of his business and still break even. This is the alternative he might very well choose.

Budgeting for profits. The third manager wanted to know how she should budget costs if business increased 20 percent. At this point, her sales are $200,000. A 20 percent increase amounts to an additional $40,000 in sales. Look at the $240,000 point on the sales line in Exhibit 8–6. Moving downward from this point, we can see that total costs would amount to about $205,000. Of this amount, $155,000 would be variable costs and $50,000 would be fixed costs. By comparing present total costs of $180,000 and her projected total costs of $205,000, it is clear that this manager would have to budget an additional $25,000 to take advantage of the opportunity for increased business.

Facing a rent hike. The fourth restaurant manager is concerned because he is facing a 20 percent rent hike. He wants to know how much he would have to increase sales in order to compensate for the rent hike and still maintain his present profit margin.

Rent is a fixed cost. We will assume that a 20 percent rent hike will produce a 10 percent rise in fixed costs. So instead of $50,000 in fixed costs, this manager may have to pay out $55,000 in fixed costs. To determine the effects of this change, we must reconstruct the break-even chart with fixed costs set at the $55,000 level and total costs at $185,000. This reconstruction is shown in Exhibit 8–7. The current profit margin is

$20,000. The reconstructed chart shows that this manager must have sales of $215,000 if he is to maintain a profit margin of $20,000. Sales must increase by $15,000 to compensate for a cost increase of $5,000.

Our examples illustrate the use of a break-even chart to solve problems with projected financial data. These restaurant managers can now make informed decisions regarding their financial problems. It is easy to see how managers could use break-even analysis to answer a variety of "What if?" questions about their businesses.

The Historical Period

In our examples, we have used historical financial data from the prior year in constructing our break-even chart. Break-even charts can also be based on historical data from semiannual, quarterly or shorter periods. In fact, break-even charts

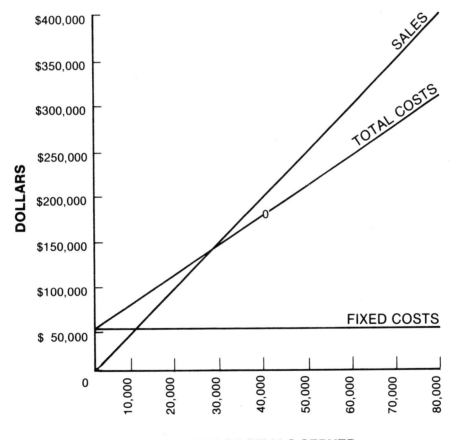

EXHIBIT 8–7   With fixed costs at $55,000.

may be based entirely on theoretical data. This would be the case if you were opening a new restaurant and had to estimate sales and costs for the upcoming period.

Reliability of Break-Even Projections

As we know, the break-even chart is used to provide projections, and projections are seldom 100 percent reliable. A forecast of tomorrow's weather is more reliable than a forecast of next week's weather. Similarly, break-even projections are more reliable the closer they are to actual historical data. One should bear this caution in mind when using break-even projections.

The break-even charts in our examples show variable costs as a straight line. This representation of variable costs is not entirely realistic. Costs per unit tend to drop as purchase quantities increase. Quantity discounts for purchases of food or beverages would decrease the rate at which variable costs rise as sales increase. As a result, profits may be understated or overstated at purchasing levels that are significantly different from actual purchasing levels. We should bear this additional caution in mind when using break-even charts.

SUMMARY

You have seen how break-even charts are constructed and interpreted. Remember this aid to financial decision-making when you have problems involving the relationships between sales, costs and profits. To help you construct break-even charts, here is a brief description of the steps.

1. Divide the vertical axis into steps up to the amount of the total sales volume in which you are interested.
2. Divide the horizontal axis into steps representing the number of average meals sold. The highest number of average meals sold will produce the maximum sales volume on the graph.
3. Graph sales by drawing a diagonal line from zero sales to maximum sales volume on the graph.
4. Determine total fixed costs and graph this quantity by drawing a horizontal line across the graph at the appropriate dollar level.
5. Circle the intersection where the total number of meals served for the historical period crosses the total cost level for the same period.
6. Draw a line between the point where fixed costs intersect the vertical dollar axis and the point representing total costs for the historical period. Extend this total cost line to the edge of the graph.

STUDY QUESTIONS

1. What three variables of vital interest to the operator of a business are plotted on the break-even chart?

2. What kind of a line represents fixed costs? Explain the slope of this line.

3. Describe briefly how variable costs are extracted from data graphed on the break-even chart.

4. In what sense does break-even analysis serve as a flexible budget?

5. Why might the variable costs line on the chart be a curve?

6. Discuss generally the reliability of break-even projections.

7. In the mathematical formula for the break-even point, *BEP* is represented as a ratio. Complete the equation:

$$BEP = \frac{FC}{(?)}$$

8. Describe how the manager in our example used the break-even chart in "biting the bullet"—cutting prices against competition.

CHAPTER 9

BUDGETING

Looking back 'aheadwards'

PURPOSE

To examine the budget as an operating plan expressed in financial terms, and as a vehicle for evaluating and controlling operations; and to see how the budget can further serve management as a personnel-motivating and training device when the budget-making process is widely shared throughout the foodservice organization.

CONTENT

Budgeting as a Management Function

Organization of the Budgeting Process

Steps in Developing the Budget

Who Should Make the Budget

When the Budget Should Be Prepared

Fixed vs. Flexible Budgeting

Typical Foodservice Budgets
    Sales forecasting
    Cost forecasting

WHY MAKE A BUDGET?

WE ORDINARILY THINK OF A BUDGET as a self-imposed schedule of expenses that will keep us within our income. In a business sense a budget is more than a plan for *spending* cash resources. Since we are in business, it becomes a plan for *using* resources of all kinds—cash, materials, tools and labor—to produce goods and services for profit. Budgeting is often described as a financial expression of the business plan. This is a fair description if we agree that a business plan seeks to project where we are going, how we propose to get there, what it will cost and what it will pay—all based on competent analysis of past operations and on the best available indicators for the future.

That seems a large order, but believe it or not we look to a budget to do even more than this. If used properly it not only *evaluates* and *plans;* it is the means of developing *controls* as we progress through the operating period projected.

We will take a further look at controls, of costs especially, but there is another purpose a budget can serve, which seems often to be neglected. Experience in working with people will show how effective the budget can be in motivating personnel. Give every department head and supervisor—indeed, every employee in the organization—an appropriate part in making the budget, in setting goals and deciding how to reach them, and you will see how everyone becomes more conscious of his or her responsibilities and takes greater pride in the company's achievements. This factor appears to be particularly significant in the restaurant industry and other "service" industries in which the people-to-people contacts are so direct and impelling, within the enterprise and between the enterprise and its customers.

Too often the budget is prepared in a perfunctory manner. The supervisor receives a memorandum from management. "Darn," he says, "budget time again! Now they expect me to do this in addition to all the other work I have to do!" Then, reaching into the file, he pulls out last year's budget, adds five percent to all the figures and sends them up to management.

THE BUDGETING PROCESS

The budget should initially be approached as a review of the past, a self-study of the previous budgetary period. As the review is made, both successes and failures will be considered. Thus the planner avails himself of seasoned, if not reasoned, information on which to base a decision to expand, curtail or otherwise change an operation. (You decide to serve breakfast and it works. Or you "discover" breakfast and decide to serve it.) Very often the decision is not a one-way or a one-time *event,* but a process combining elements of look-and-find with find-and-keep. Which came first will not always be clear. As our learned colleagues would say, the process is iterative. In any case, once the budget is adopted it can provide insights for the development of controls and should be used in this way.

Using historical data, then, and the best predictions (see Chapter 13) that can be mustered, we draw up a plan of action which may reasonably be expected to bring about the optimum operation for our foodservice company. Translated into monetary terms by the budget, this business plan can now be monitored by the accounting process to show how closely the company comes to its objectives. Since the budget is a projection, it must of course be prepared in advance of the operating period being projected. Budgets might be prepared for various time periods in a foodservice operation. A budget may be designed to cover operations for the entire year, for a month, a week, or for only one day. When we think of preparing budgets, we normally think of the income and expenses of the organization. In preparing a yearly budget, therefore, the entire sales for the period and all operating expenses are projected. Our present study deals mainly with operations of the enterprise, so the kind of budget with which we are most concerned is that usually referred to as an *operating budget.*

In contrast to a yearly budget, a daily budget might only project the number of meals to be served, or the number of specific entrées (X number of ribeye steaks, Y number of roast beef servings). Or it may be used simply to plan the number of waitresses needed for the day. The purpose of the annual budget most likely will be to predict the amount of profit the foodservice operation will yield during the fiscal period. The object of a short-term budget would ordinarily be to estimate the amount of food and size of staff required to handle the trade in an immediate operating period.

USING THE BUDGET

Preparation of the annual budget is an extremely important function, but one must be careful not to think that preparing the budget is the complete process. Anticipated results should be compared with the actual performance when the period is over. To say this another way, we must estimate before the fiscal period how much will be sold and what the relationship between expenses and sales will be. Then it is important to note at the close of the fiscal period whether we sold as much or more than anticipated, and whether expenses were higher or lower than projected.

The use of the budget as an accounting device and management tool does not stop at this point. Each item appearing on the budget should be analyzed. If sales were less than anticipated, management should try to find out why. A deviation from the projection may be easily explained by a siege of unfavorable weather, or by a recession in the economy causing people to limit their travel. A local strike or change in traffic pattern during road repairs could bring an unforeseeable drop in sales. Or the reason may be closer to home: indifferent service, inferior food preparation, a lapse in good housekeeping. It is important to find out as soon as possible why your business objectives are not being met, so that corrective measures can be taken.

It is no less imperative to analyze expenses than it is to analyze sales. If a labor expense of $4,000 for the month has been projected, and $5,000 is spent, immediate action to reduce labor costs, or to check your estimate, is in order. If food costs of $50,000 were projected and the actual cost of food for the month was $60,000, prompt investigation is clearly indicated. The first task facing management is to identify the problem, if one exists, and to define it. Thereafter, the inevitable question is what to do about it. The happy condition may arise that an observed increase in dollars paid for merchandise is explained by an increase in sales; if, however, expenses have risen in the face of unchanging or, even worse, declining sales, it is time to take a close look. Every possibility of high food cost (as discussed in Chapter 14) must be investigated and acted upon. Deviation of actual costs from budgeted costs may be relatively easy to explain, independent of sales. It may be that food supplies were not available from the normal source, and the new source charged substantially higher prices. Because of an inflation spiral, food prices during a given period may have taken an abnormally large jump. Perhaps changes in personnel or lack of supervision have resulted in excessive waste, or pilferage. An informed management, knowing the real cause of a problem, can quickly take corrective action. The evidence may suggest changing purveyors, improving methods of control, upgrading employee training, modifying recipes (using less-expensive ingredients), or adjusting portion sizes and menu prices. The solution will often involve one or more such decisions.

A caution. We have been emphasizing the virtue of the budget and its proper use. It is only fair to add that management should avoid becoming a slave to a budget. The business world is a dynamic environment and those who manage a business must recognize that the budget is a control device in their hands, not a strait jacket on their freedom of action. As conditions change, so must the budget change and relate to new conditions. Predictions are always based on assumptions, so it must be acknowledged that elements of error may intrude on the best of plans. Shortening the budget period or organizing it in time segments, e.g., dividing the yearly budget into monthly periods, will reduce the effect of divergencies and make them easier to manage.

In sum, the budget is to be regarded as a vehicle for planning, control and evaluation, giving management a better grasp of sales and expenses and leading to greater profits. If it is not developed and used in this way it is likely to become little more than a paper exercise.

WHO SHOULD MAKE THE BUDGET?

Budget-making as we have conceived it closely parallels business planning. Primary responsibility naturally resides with top management, but the budgetary process flows up and down along the chain of command—the channels of management. Since the budget for a significant operating period will focus on income and expense, the people directly concerned with development of sales and with control of expenses would appear to have the basic responsibility. But who in a foodservice or other business enterprise is not involved one way or other with revenues and the cost of doing business? And let's not forget our premise that the budget can serve as a powerful motivator of personnel.

If, however, we want to be systematic and consider how this cooperative effort is to be organized, we may say that:

1. Top management sets the goals.
2. Department heads develop plans to reach those goals.
3. The accountants translate these plans into dollars.

But that is a picture painted with a broad brush. Many details are missing, along with some important background features. We would have to add something like:

4. . . . And the cooks, waitresses and busboys take part in these plans so they will be gung ho to make them happen.

That's the idea, all right, but we would also have to add that top management consulted with its accountants in the first place with questions like, "Where do we stand today? How much can we commit to redesigning the dining room, expanding kitchen facilities and . . . ?" And we would have to spell out how department heads consulted with their supervisors, and the supervisors with their workers, to make item 4 come to pass. We would, in fact, have to point out that the whole process is an intricate one, involving all hands in a repeated cycle of trial and error, backing and filling, all along the line, each cycle approximating the final solution a little more closely. We would find that it was, indeed, a process deserving the sophisticated adjective "iterative."

For example, considering the typical organization of a rather large foodservice operation: The catering manager would project the number of persons to be fed during the fiscal period; given this sales prediction, the chef would estimate the quantity of food necessary (see Chapter 14); the purchasing agent now computes the dollar cost of the merchandise, the personnel manager figures the size of staff required, and from all of this the accounting department is able to advise management how revenues and expenses will tally out, and what the profit will be. In a smaller restaurant organization, many of the functions formally assigned in our example would be concentrated in the duties of a few people, but the principle is the same.

Not only will all-hands budget-making provide incentives for the staff, it can also be a very effective training technique. When management shares its planning and evaluation functions with supervisors at all levels, and these supervisors go to the individual members of their working staffs for information and suggestions, the budget becomes an integrated communication system. How this system serves to promote indoctrination and training will be seen from the above example. You can yourself extend this budget-sharing procedure in a number of ways, showing, for instance, how the service supervisor would meet with waiters and waitresses, busboys and other personnel under his or her direction, explaining the purpose of the budget and encouraging them to come up with ideas for improving sales and reducing costs. The point to recognize is that many people are employed in so-called entry-level

ABC Foodservice Company
BUDGET
Year Ending Dec. 31, 19xx

SALES		
Food	$100,000	
Beverages	50,000	
Gross Sales	150,000	100%
COST OF SALES		
Food	40,000	40
Beverage	15,000	30
Total Cost of Sales	55,000	36.7
Gross Profit	95,000	63.3
CONTROLLABLE EXPENSE		
Salaries (including employee meals)	45,000	30.0
Payroll taxes	4,500	3.0
Laundry	3,750	2.5
Utilities (heat, light, power)	4,875	3.25
China, glassware, silver	4,500	3.0
Supplies	5,250	3.5
Advertising	3,000	2.0
Insurance	2,250	1.5
License & taxes	1,500	1.0
Office expenses	3,000	2.0
Sundry expenses	3,750	2.5
Total Controllable Expense	81,375	54.25
Profit before Occupancy costs	13,625	9.0
OCCUPANCY COSTS		
Rent, insurance, taxes	7,500	5.0
Profit before federal income tax	$ 6,125	4.0%

EXHIBIT 9–1 Example of a fixed budget, based on one sales projection. Figures are hypothetical.

jobs for a long time, and appreciate being recognized and given an opportunity to show their interest in the success of the organization. These people are in a very real sense on the firing line for sales, customer relations and cost control, and using the budget to make them more aware of their importance can be a powerful factor in the growth of the business.

Information generated in this way can now be correlated and put in standard budget format by the accounting department. Top management may then see fit to refer this planning package to a budget committee composed of department heads and other responsible persons for review. Evaluating each item from a detached viewpoint, the committee presents final recommendations to management.

TIMING THE BUDGET

Since the budget is a planning device, the lead time necessary for its preparation must first be decided. The period of time to be covered by the budget is an important factor. It will of course take longer to budget for a year than for a month. Two other conflicting considerations will require keen judgment on management's part: (1) The budget must be prepared far enough in advance to allow for well-founded projections; and (2) it must be prepared close enough to the fiscal period involved so that recent events may be taken into consideration.

FIXED AND FLEXIBLE BUDGETS

The company may select one of two basic types of budgets—the fixed operating budget, or the variable (flexible) budget —and this choice will affect the planning time allowed. The fixed operating budget is developed by projecting one level of sales and developing expenses based on these sales. The variable budget projects two or more levels of sales with their corresponding estimates of expense.

The fixed budget is quite reliable when there is a limited fluctuation in sales, as may be the case in a hospital or other institutional foodservice. Industrial feeding establishments with a fairly predictable pattern of sales may also use the fixed operating budget to good advantage (see Exhibit 9–1).

In contrast, flexible budgeting is a likely route for foodservice organizations that find their sales to have been erratic, and for planners of new operations with no historical figures to guide them. Let's suppose, for example, that in making the budget study the managers find their sales have been unpredictable. Their thinking might go something like this: "All our calculations indicate that business in the coming year should reach a sales volume of $150,000. However, we know business in the past has been unsteady. So what will happen to expenses if sales should drop to $135,000? Or what if we find ourselves with a good year and have a volume of $165,000? In order to make good decisions and keep our business under control, we need to know how expenses will relate to sales at these various levels. So, we will use $150,000 as the base level, and construct budgets for that level, and for 10 percent below and 10 percent above that level. This should provide us with ample information for deciding as we go along."

ABC Foodservice Company
BUDGET
Year Ending Dec. 31, 19xx

	90%		100%		110%	
SALES						
Food	$ 90,000		$100,000		$110,000	
Beverages	45,000		50,000		55,000	
Gross Sales	135,000		150,000		165,000	
COST OF SALES						
Food	36,000	40%	40,000	40%	44,000	40%
Beverages	13,500	30	15,000	30	16,500	30
Total Cost of Sales	49,500		55,000		60,500	
Gross Profit	85,000		95,000		105,500	
CONTROLLABLE EXPENSE						
Salaries	40,500	30	45,000	30	46,200	28
Payroll taxes	4,050	3	4,500	3	4,620	2.8
Laundry	3,375	2.5	3,750	2.5	4,950	3
Utilities	4,725	3.5	4,875	3.25	4,950	3
China, glassware, silver	4,050	3	4,500	3	4,950	3
Supplies	4,725	3.5	5,250	3.5	4,950	3
Advertising	2,025	1.5	3,000	2	3,300	2
Insurance	1,350	1	2,250	1.5	2,475	1.5
License & taxes	1,350	1	1,500	1	1,650	1
Office expenses	2,700	2	3,000	2	2,475	1.5
Sundry expenses	3,375	2.5	3,750	2.5	4,125	2.5
Total Controllable Expense	72,225	53.5	81,375	54.2	84,645	51.3
Profit before Occupancy Costs	13,275	9.8	13,625	9.08	20,855	12.6
OCCUPANCY COSTS	7,500	5.55	7,500	5.0	7,500	4.54
Profit before federal income tax	$ 5,775	4.25%	$ 6,125	4.08%	$ 13,355	8.06%

EXHIBIT 9–2 A variable budget, projecting three possible sales levels. Figures are hypothetical.

The flexible budget is really two, three or more budgets in one, and is therefore more complex and time-consuming. But it can save time and can help in decision-making in a fluctuating market (see Exhibit 9–2).

TYPICAL FOODSERVICE BUDGETS

There is no strict standard for the budget format. Exhibit 9–3 shows one of many forms used by foodservice operations. Since sales may vary widely, in reaction to seasonal and other factors, and because it is easier to plan for shorter periods, the budget is usually divided into monthly segments. The budget format illustrated here also has columns for the third and fifth years, which management may want to show in making long-range plans.

For control purposes, also, it is well to break the annual budget into smaller units. Most companies find that the month is a convenient time period both for accounting and budgeting. Once annual sales goals have been established, monthly sales figures can be developed by casting monthly sales in the previous year as percentages of gross sales for that year. Suppose, for example, that annual sales for the coming year have been budgeted at $150,000. To determine what portion of that amount will be produced in the month of January, sales for the previous year will be examined. The previous January produced 7.25 percent of the gross business for the year, and for this reason it might be reasonable to expect that January of the coming year will likewise produce 7.25 percent of the sales volume, or $10,865. Each month is examined in this fashion and fitted into the budget for the coming year (see Exhibit 9–4, p. 114).

Sales Forecasting

As indicated, anticipating sales (revenue) is the first step in the budget-making process. It is also the most important step since all expense is related to sales volume. The budget-maker gets his information for forecasting sales from two sources: historical data (on business experiences of the past) and anticipated data (on events the planner expects to occur in the future). The historical data is derived from sales records. It is important that these records be kept in accurate detail. Not only are dollar sales figures of interest; so are other sales analysis data, including the number of customers, average check size and performance of particular menu items. Various factors affecting sales—weather, business and social activities, holidays and other seasonal events—should also be noted. The effect of local industrial happenings (plant openings and closings), housing development or clearance projects, road construction, and the like, should likewise be studied, as well as legislative changes that might cause deviations from normal business volume. General economic trends should be noted and analyzed. For example, the dollar volume of sales may increase while the customer count remains constant or even declines, because of increased menu prices reflecting dollar inflation.

Cost Forecasting

Cost forecasting seeks to determine the expense that will be generated in

BUDGET — Year ending 19_____

	JANUARY		FEBRUARY		MARCH		APRIL		MAY		JUNE		
	Amount	%	Amount	%	Amount	%	Amount	%	Amount	%	Amount	%	
SALES													
Food													
Beverage													
Total sales													
COST OF SALES													
Food													
Beverage													
Total cost of sales													
GROSS PROFIT _ _ _ _ _													
CONTROLLABLE EXPENSES													
Wages													
Management salaries													
Employee benefits													
Supplies													
Replacements													
Laundry													
Utilities													
Cleaning & sanitation													
Maintenance													
Advertising													
Administration													
Total controllable													
FIXED EXPENSES													
Rent													
Depreciation													
Other occupancy exp.													
Other fixed expense													
Total fixed expense													
Total expenses													
NET PROFIT OR (LOSS) _ _													

EXHIBIT 9–3   Sample format for a foodservice budget.

	JULY		AUGUST		SEPTEMBER		OCTOBER		NOVEMBER		DECEMBER		TOTAL FIRST YR.		THIRD YR. 19___		FIFTH YR. 19___	
	Amount	%	Amount	%	Amount	%	Amount	%	Amount	%	Amount	%	Amount	%	Amount	%	Amount	%

Prepared by:

producing sales. As with sales, the budgetmaker begins the projections of cost by looking at the record, with the idea that established trends will continue in the future. He considers, for example, federal and state taxes, union contracts, and economic pressures that affect wages. Does he have any reason to think that these factors will change? That is the

MONTHLY SALES TABULATION

Food sales for the year		$ 80,000
Beverage sales for the year		40,000
Total annual sales		$120,000

Month	Food Sales		Beverage Sales
Jan.	$ 5,500	7.25%	$ 2,750
Feb.	6,000	7.50	3,000
Mar.	6,500	8.25	3,250
April	6,500	8.25	3,250
May	6,750	8.50	3,275
June	7,000	8.00	3,500
July	7,250	9.00	3,625
Aug.	9,000	11.00	4,500
Sept.	8,500	10.00	4,250
Oct.	6,250	8.00	3,175
Nov.	5,500	7.25	2,750
Dec.	5,250	7.00	2,625
Totals	$80,000	100%	$40,000

EXHIBIT 9–4   A hypothetical analysis of annual sales, illustrating how percentages can be tabulated for monthly sales projections in next year's budget. In this example beverage sales are shown as maintaining a constant 2-to-1 ratio with food sales, a relationship that holds true in many establishments, assuming no change in menu or style of operation.

question, and often it is complicated by purely local labor conditions.

In projecting sales the planner estimates the number of patrons the foodservice can anticipate and as nearly as possible the number of specific meals to be served. Based on these estimates, food costs can be predicted with some reliability. Since food and labor represent major costs, the accuracy with which they are forecast is of utmost importance.

Management has a significant degree of control over expenditures for food and beverages, but these are also the costs that undergo wide market variations, and will therefore claim a great amount of time and effort. Expenses related to payroll—Social Security payments, unemployment insurance, workmen's compensation and related benefits—are relatively simple to compute once the payroll has been determined. Occupancy costs—rent, property taxes, depreciation, insurance on property and interest on loans—can usually be estimated quite accurately. Direct operating expenses, although they do vary and may be less controllable, usually remain constant enough to allow the budget-maker to use percentages based on historical figures.

The cost of employee meals is an item of some consequence in the budget of many foodservices. Under the *Uniform System of Accounts for Restaurants* discussed in Chapter 6, these meals are treated as a separate expense. Their importance depends on the type of operation. The cost involved can be substantial, and some operators figure it very closely. Others determine an average cost per employee or sales dollar and use this figure in their budget analyses.

Increasing sales will often reduce the unit cost of food and indirectly reduce the cost of labor, but volume does not solve all problems. It may in some instances aggravate them. Budget studies must therefore consider all available data in arriving at planning factors for personnel and material.

SUMMARY

The budget is a financial expression of the operating plan of a business or other organization for a specified period of time. It is based on past performance and on assumptions for the future. Individuals at all levels of responsibility should be involved in making the budget. The budget becomes also a control device for management, as deviations from the operating plan are noted, analyzed and corrected or compensated. Management should recognize that just as the business itself must be continuously responsive to changing market conditions, the budget must be dynamic and adaptable.

"Budget time" should be looked upon as an occasion for self-study of the foodservice organization and its operations. It is a time for "looking back *aheadwards*" and should involve as many of the employees as possible.

Numerous successful organizations have found it to be a powerful instrument in educating and motivating personnel. By itself the budget is only a plan, no matter how well conceived. With all hands participating in its development and in its execution, it becomes the blueprint for a profitable operation.

The budget is developed in two basic ways: (1) from a fixed operating plan; and (2) from a flexible plan geared for a variety of operating conditions. The fixed budget is based on one sales projection. The variable budget is actually a series of budgets based on several possible levels of sales activity.

STUDY QUESTIONS

1. Consider our concept of the budget and its origin. How would you define it in a few words?
2. Who should participate in developing the budget? Discuss.
3. Describe briefly the problem we face in deciding *when* to make a budget.
4. What do we mean by a fixed operating budget?
5. What is the purpose of a flexible budget? Describe briefly.
6. Discuss at some length how the budget is used as a *control* device by management.

7. From our discussions, how do you see the budget operating as a training device?

8. Now, if you had to use *one* word, what would you call a budget? Justify this one-word concept.

PART FOUR

OWNERSHIP, CAPITAL
AND FINANCIAL DECISIONS

CHAPTER 10

FORMS OF BUSINESS ORGANIZATION

From sole ownership to the company with a 'soul' of its own

PURPOSE

To examine the types of business ownership and organization with a view to understanding how its basic constitution affects the financial management of a foodservice enterprise.

CONTENT

Why the Form of Ownership Matters

The Proprietorship
    Flexibility
    Limited leadership
    Tax position
    Unlimited liability
    Financial limitations

The Partnership
    Financial advantages
    Leadership aspects
    Unlimited liability
    The partnership agreement

The Corporation
    Limited liability
    Public ownership
    Financial advantages
    Taxability

To Incorporate or Not: The Trade-Offs

THE WAY IN WHICH A BUSINESS FIRM IS constituted, with respect to who owns and directs it, profoundly influences the way it is managed financially. The nature of its ownership has a direct bearing on the kind of income statement to be issued and on other aspects of accounting procedure to be followed. The subject is a large one and our present survey need not examine, for example, the *entity* versus the *proprietorship* theory in treating the equities of a corporation, but we *are* interested in the basic forms of ownership and their effect on operations and planning. Let us look at a typical case.

Joe Williams, the sole owner of a suburban restaurant, has been fairly successful in his operation of the business over the years. Recently occupied housing developments in his area have greatly increased his patronage potential. Joe wants to increase his seating capacity from 100 to 250. In addition, he needs new kitchen equipment in order to handle the increased volume of business he expects. He needs more capital, but he is facing a tight money market. Because of insufficient collateral, Joe is unable to obtain a loan. To raise capital for the expansion, Joe is considering sharing his ownership of the restaurant. His problem: Which would be more advantageous, a partnership or a corporation?

The following review of the common types of business organization will give us the basis for an answer to Joe Williams's problem. We will see the ad-

vantages and disadvantages of sole ownership, partnership, and corporate ownership. We will learn about the kind of trade-offs faced by a person in Joe's position, and the choices open to the founder of a restaurant business in selecting the ownership organization best adapted to its needs.

THE PROPRIETORSHIP

A proprietorship, often called a sole proprietorship, is an unincorporated business owned by *one* individual. In the accounting world the term proprietorship is also used, in a general sense, to mean ownership. Thus a single owner is said to have sole proprietorship of the capital assets of the business.

An advantage of sole ownership is flexibility—the capacity for quick response to changing conditions. In reaching decisions and in acting upon them, the sole owner is under no obligation to consult with co-owners or a board of directors, and is not bound by any policies other than those that are self-imposed. The sole owner has freedom of action in reaching financial decisions and in managing the operations of the business. If informed and wise decisions are made, the sole owner benefits from those decisions. On the other hand, if a sole owner lacks adequate knowledge, experience or judgment to make sound business decisions, he or she must live with the consequences.

The proprietor of a restaurant may

have limited knowledge or ability in one or more areas of management, and this will limit the success and growth of the business. Where ownership is shared, as is the case with the corporation or partnership, specialization tends to develop and the business as a whole gains a competitive advantage through the efficiencies of specialization.

In the proprietorship, the proprietor is personally liable for all the indebtedness incurred by the business. If a restaurant should suffer financial loss and be unable to pay its creditors, the personal assets of the proprietor may be claimed by the creditors to satisfy obligations created in the course of business. In other words, the sole owner has "unlimited liability." The fact that a restaurant owner is personally liable for all obligations may have a limiting effect on the size of the restaurant operation. As proprietorships become larger through expansion and growth, owners frequently change the form of ownership and limit their liability through incorporation.

Among the liabilities assumed by the owner of a proprietorship is that of taxes. The proprietor pays income taxes on the profits generated by the business. For tax purposes, it makes no difference what a restaurant proprietor does with profits. They may be withdrawn as personal income or reinvested in the restaurant, in whole or in part. In any case the proprietor must pay taxes on the profits as if they were personal income.

Although a restaurant owner gets no tax advantage through the reinvestment of profits, the restaurant can only grow as a business to the extent that the proprietor reinvests profits or borrows money. This limitation in available means of financing tends to slow the rate of business growth. As you recall, Joe Williams was considering a change in the form of his business to obtain enough capital to take advantage of opportunities for growth. Usually a sole owner invests all available personal resources in the enterprise when it is first established. As a result, unless the owner develops other sources of assets, the growth of the business depends on the reinvestment of profits, i.e., on internal financing. This method of financing obviously limits the rate at which the business can grow.

A proprietorship survives only as long as the owner. A proprietorship is generally under the active management of the owner. When that active management ceases, the business itself may have to be dissolved. Should the proprietor suffer from some disability that limits his or her capacity to manage the business, the business itself might suffer and even cease to exist. In most cases, a proprietorship shares the owner's vulnerability. As a result, it may lack the continuity and capacity for survival of other forms of business.

THE PARTNERSHIP

A partnership is an unincorporated business owned by *two or more* individuals. The difference between a partnership and a proprietorship is in the number of owners. Since there are more owners in a partnership, more individuals are available to participate in the financing of the business. The source of contributions to capital are increased and the possibility of growth is increased. (Frequently, proprietorships fail because they are undercapitalized. They have insufficient reserve capital to tide them through financial emergencies or occasional lulls in business income.) In this respect, partnerships have a distinct financial advantage over proprietorships.

Since the partnership has more than one owner, the possibility of specialization in management is also enhanced. This could be quite helpful in the operation of a restaurant where one partner acts as cook and manages the kitchen, while the other partner specializes in management of service to patrons. As a restaurant business grows, partners might be found who can contribute specialized knowledge in the area of financial management or administration. The fact that a business is under the direct and close supervision of owners may very well increase the efficiency of its operations.

As with the proprietorship, one of the disadvantages of the partnership is the unlimited financial liability devolving on the owners. In a general partnership, each of the general partners is fully liable for all of the debts of the company. If a partnership is liquidated with outstanding debts, either or both of the partners are liable for the full amount. Even if partners have contributed unequal amounts in capitalizing the partnership, each partner is fully liable for all of the debts of the partnership. And this liability extends to the personal assets of the partners.

The partnership, as a business entity, does not pay a federal income tax. The partners, as individuals, pay federal income tax on their individual net income

from the partnership. All profits, whether they are withdrawn by the owners or left in the company, are taxed, and partners individually pay income tax on their proportionate share of those profits.

Because one partner is financially liable for the actions of the other, a relationship of trust and confidence in their mutual responsibility is necessary for the successful conduct of the business. Because they will be working closely together, partners should have compatible personalities. These requirements of a successful partnership should be carefully considered when it is being formed.

Partnerships have been formed between individuals who regarded each other as friends. After working together over a period of time, differences of opinion in the management of the business develop and the partners are unable to work together amicably. Eventually, issues may develop which produce unreconcilable differences between the two partners. In such circumstances, one partner may wish to acquire the interests of the other. Of course, either partner may refuse to sell his proportionate share of the partnership. If neither partner wishes to sell, it may be necessary to dissolve the partnership, with each partner taking his proportionate share of the assets.

In order to prevent subsequent misunderstandings and disagreements, the business relationship between the partners should be described in a partnership agreement drawn up with the assistance of legal counsel. Most articles of partnership specify, at the minimum, the following information and conditions:

1. The name of the partnership.

2. The nature of the goods or services to be provided by the company.
3. The location of the business.
4. The period of time for which the company is going to operate.
5. The owners of the company.
6. How profits of the company are to be distributed to each partner.
7. The different business or managerial responsibilities of the partners.
8. The means by which the partnership can be dissolved if irreconcilable differences should develop.
9. The amount of vacation time, sick leave and similar rights and benefits each partner is to have.

It is important that articles of partnership be drawn up at the very beginning. In some cases, partners have waited until disagreements have arisen before delineating their business relationship in formal terms. It is difficult to obtain agreement on details of the business relationship to be specified in articles of partnership after conflicting interests have developed between partners. If prospective partners cannot agree upon the specific nature of their mutual obligations and responsibilities at the outset of a partnership, it is obvious that they will be unable to do so after they have committed funds and effort, and are involved in business operations.

Death, insolvency, or mental incompetence of one of the partners results in the legal dissolution of the partnership. That its legal existence depends on the life and condition of any one of the partners may be a serious shortcoming. The partnership is similar to the proprietorship in that it lacks the continuity and survival capability enjoyed by a corporation. This disadvantage tends to limit the growth of a partnership.

THE CORPORATION

A corporation is a legal entity apart from its owners, created, and authorized to operate, by state charter. In both a proprietorship and a partnership, the owners are entitled to the net assets and are liable for the debts of the business. However, the owners of a corporation are not liable for the debts incurred by the corporation. The state has granted the corporation authority to enter into legal contracts. Accordingly, the corporation is responsible for its own indebtedness.

An obvious advantage of the corporate form of business organization is the limited liability of the owners. The creditors of a corporation may claim the assets of the corporation to satisfy business debts, but they may not claim the personal assets of the individual owners of the corporation. A stockholder of a corporation risks only his investment in the corporation.

Through the sale of stock, it is possible for the corporation to obtain capital funds that, to the individual investors, represent small contributions, but which, in the aggregate, represent a very large amount and provide a strong financial base. The ability to gather capital in this manner gives the corporation a competitive advantage over proprietorships and partnerships in growth potential.

Stockholders influence the management of the corporation through the election of directors. Usually, each stockholder is entitled to one vote for each share of stock held. The board of directors is responsible to the stockholders for the profitable performance of the corporation as a business. The board of directors selects and controls the business specialists who manage the operation. This form of business organization therefore permits individuals with available capital, but who lack the time or talent to manage it, to invest in a potentially profitable enterprise.

Stability of the corporation as a legal and business entity is relatively more assured. The financial condition, the mental and physical health, or the death, of stockholders does not affect the life of the corporation. Stock ownership can pass freely from individual to individual through public or private transactions. If stockholders so desire, the corporation as a whole may be sold or it may be liquidated and the proceeds distributed to the stockholders. It is possible for a corporation to declare bankruptcy and go out of business. In such a situation, creditors have a claim upon the assets of the corporation, but no claim against the personal assets of the stockholders.

With certain exceptions, the earnings of a corporation are subject to income tax. After the corporation has paid income tax on profits, the after-tax, net income of the corporation may be distributed to the stockholders as dividends. On the other hand, the corporation may elect to retain all or part of its earnings for internal reinvestment. Dividends received by the stockholders are subject to the individual income tax.

Forming a corporation involves more complicated procedures and expense than forming a proprietorship or partnership. Usually the founders of a corporation require legal assistance in preparing the necessary documents required by the state and in obtaining authorization to operate in the state. Corporate operations must meet certain requirements set up by the state. These cover such matters as regular meetings of the board of directors, recording the minutes of board and stockholder meetings, and preparing and maintaining certain records required by state laws governing corporations.

Some states require corporations to pay state income tax or require a regular franchise tax for the privilege of operating a corporation within the state. These taxes may be modest or large, depending on the size of the corporation and the scope of its activities.

In comparison to a proprietorship or partnership, a corporation enjoys two advantages: the generally greater ease with which it can raise capital through the sale of stock, and the limited liability of the owners of the corporation—the stockholders. While the owners of a proprietorship or partnership are personally liable for all of the debts of the business, the stockholder is only liable to the extent of his investment in the corporation. While proprietorships and partnerships are not taxed as business entities apart from their owners, corporations do pay income tax. Since corporations tend to be better capitalized in comparison with proprietorships and partnerships, they find it easier to hire the services of professional managers. Although organizing a corporation is more complicated and costly than founding a proprietorship or partnership, the benefits of incorporation usually outweigh this disadvantage.

THE TRADE-OFFS

As you will recall, Joe Williams, the restaurant proprietor, needed to raise capital in order to take advantage of opportunities for growth of his restaurant. Having reviewed the different forms of business organization, we are now aware of the trade-offs that Joe Williams faces in raising capital by sharing ownership of his restaurant. If he asks a partner to buy into the restaurant, he must be certain that he can work amicably with that partner for as far as he can see into the future. He must find somebody who can contribute to the management of the restaurant, and he must find someone who is financially responsible. Joe would have to assume full financial responsibilities for the actions of his partner should he elect to form a partnership.

If he wishes to raise capital through the formation of a corporation, he must locate persons who are willing to purchase shares in that corporation. In addition, he must undertake the legal procedures required by the state for the formation of the corporation and satisfy certain state requirements in the continuing operation of the corporation. As a sole owner, Joe is currently liable to the full extent of his personal assets for the debts incurred in the operation of his restaurant. Should he incorporate, he will possess the real advantage of limited liability in case the expected growth of his business does not materialize and the corporation must liquidate.

It is possible that if his restaurant continues to be successful, Joe will change the form of ownership from a proprietorship to a partnership, and finally to that of a corporation. Most restaurants are begun as one-owner establishments. Many of the more successful restaurants have evolved from proprietorships to partnerships and then to corporations. One study indicates that restaurants with an annual sales volume of $700,000 and above typically rely upon the corporate form of business organization.

SUMMARY

The form of ownership has important effects on the financial affairs of a business enterprise. It may be the controlling factor in the size of the business, and it is sure to influence the way its books are kept. The *proprietorship* has the advantage of flexibility. The sole owner can rapidly take advantage of business opportunities insofar as he has the ability and financial capacity to do so. He enjoys the full rewards of his efforts but must also bear unlimited liability. If his business should fail, creditors may claim the personal assets of the proprietor to satisfy business debts. The proprietorship frequently lacks the degree of managerial specialization enjoyed by other forms of business organization. This lack of specialization in management tends to place the proprietorship at a competitive disadvantage. The profits of a one-owner business are taxed as his personal income, and the growth of a proprietorship is often limited to the reinvestment of those profits. Finally, a proprietorship as a legal entity survives only as long as the owner. Accordingly, the proprietorship lacks the continuity enjoyed by other forms of business organization.

The *partnership* has greater financing potential than the proprietorship because there is more than one owner to contribute capital. The possibility also exists for specialization of the partners in different aspects of management or business operation. This may result in closer supervision and more efficient operations than could be achieved in a proprietorship. A disadvantage of the partnership is its unlimited liability for the partners. Each partner is liable for all of the debts of the business and the personal assets of each partner may be claimed by creditors in satisfying those debts. Each partner pays an individual income tax on his proportionate share of the profits, but the partnership as a business entity is not subject to income tax. For the successful operation of a partnership, the partners must be compatible and share a clear understanding of their business relationship and their specific obligations and responsibilities. The nature of the business relationship and the obligations and responsibilities of the partners should be spelled out in a partnership agreement. Finally, a partnership is dissolved by the death, insolvency, or mental incompetence of any one of the partners. For this reason, the partnership lacks the stability and continuity of a corporation.

The *corporation* enjoys two advantages over a proprietorship or partnership—the ease with which it can raise capital through the sale of stock, and the limited liability of its owners, the stockholders. While the owners of a proprietorship or partnership are personally liable for all debts of the business, the stockholder is only liable to the extent of his or her investment in the corporation. While proprietorships and partnerships are not taxed as business entities, corporations do pay taxes as separately constituted bodies under the law. Since corporations tend to be better capitalized, they find it easier to hire the services of professional managers. The formation of a corporation is more complicated and costly, but the benefits of incorporation usually make it worthwhile.

STUDY QUESTIONS

1. What are the major advantages of a proprietorship?
2. Describe the limitations which may face a typical proprietor seeking to expand his business operation.
3. What are the likely disadvantages of the partnership as a form of business ownership-organization?
4. Name four of the *conditions* which should be specified in a partnership agreement.
5. How does a corporation differ essentially from a proprietorship or partnership?

6. Trace the lines of financial responsibility connecting the stockholders, the directors, and the managers of a corporation. Are the lines of authority different?

7. What source of capital is open to a corporation that is not open to a business firm more simply constituted? What source is common to all?

8. Contrast the ways in which the earnings of a proprietorship and those of a corporation are taxed.

CHAPTER 11

METHODS OF FINANCING

How to get, use and track operating funds

PURPOSE

To explore the methods whereby corporations finance their operations in the long and the short run, and to see how these transactions are accounted for in the statement of changes in financial position (cash statement), a necessary follow-up of the balance sheet and the income & expense statement.

CONTENT

Function of the Cash Statement

Solvency and Cash Management

Sources of Funds
    Stocks
        Common stock
        Preferred stock
    Bonds
    Retained earnings
    The franchise

The Feasibility Study

PEOPLE IN BUSINESS need many tools for a successful operation. Just as the gardener uses the hoe and spade, yet also requires other tools for specialized work, so does the business operator need many implements to get the job done. As the business grows and becomes more complex, so must these tools be refined to serve special purposes. Most managers are satisfied with the information presented to them on the income & expense statement and on the balance sheet. But when the operation expands, the manager becomes farther removed from the work going on in any particular department and must rely to a greater extent on reports from subordinates. These reports may take the form of schedules and exhibits supporting the figures in one of the basic accounting statements discussed earlier. Or they may be reports he requires now but didn't require previously when he supervised those activities in person. Among the additional statements bringing more detailed information to a more remote manager is the *statement of changes in financial position,* which explains the changes in working capital (or cash).

CHANGES IN FINANCIAL POSITION

The balance sheet, as we know, shows the financial condition of the company at a particular instant. The statement of changes in financial position indicates the changes that have occurred in the various balance sheet accounts over a period leading up to that instant. In large companies that find it necessary to project their operations into the future, this statement is a highly useful instrument. Knowing the source of funds and their application, and knowing their effect on liabilities, assets and capital, is important in long-range planning. Management of cash is always vital to the company's operations and may be of immediate concern.

Basically, the statement of changes in financial position explains all sources of cash, lists all applications of cash, and shows the net increase or decrease in cash for the fiscal period. We have previously seen that, when basing the income statement on accrual accounting, the method of handling cash does not affect income or expense. This points up the need for the statement of changes in financial position because it is essential for management to know the cash activity and position of the company. You will also recall that the income statement does not differentiate between cash sales and sales made on account, and does not show whether expenses represent immediate or deferred transfer of cash. The income statement shows *all* income and expenses regardless of whether these accounts increase cash, decrease cash or have no effect on cash. The importance of this is that management must be certain that the company has on hand, at all times, sufficient cash to pay debts as they mature.

130

The Cash Statement

Up to this point we have been using formal accounting terminology and calling the statement of changes in financial position by its proper name. This statement is often informally called the funds statement, which relates it to working capital (*all* working funds). But for purposes of brevity, and since in this chapter we emphasize the cash concept, we will refer to the statement of changes in financial position as the *cash statement*.

Management must know why money was received and why money was spent, since it is concerned with the profitability of the company. This information is contained in the income statement. Management is also concerned with the financial position of the company at a given moment. Stated another way, management must know what the company owns, what it owes and what its net worth is, and this information is presented on the balance sheet. Management is further concerned with owners' equity for the fiscal period, and this information is given on the capital statement, otherwise known as the statement of retained earnings. It is evident that none of these three financial statements tries to summarize in any fashion the collection and disbursement of cash. It is therefore necessary to introduce the cash statement. Its contents are outlined here in abbreviated form:

CASH STATEMENT

Sources of Cash
From Operations	$_____
Other Sources	_____
Total	_____
Less Applications of Cash	$_____
Net Increase or Decrease in Cash	$_____

This simple outline shows the basic content of the cash statement, how it lists sources of cash, subtracts cash used and indicates the net change in cash position. Refer now to Exhibit 11–1 for further description of the elements of this statement.

The line in Exhibit 11–1, sources from operations, accounts for the increase in cash caused by business activity during the fiscal period. It represents the total cash collected in that period, irrespective of when the income was generated, and does not necessarily show *all* cash *collectable* for that period. Some incomes billed in the fiscal period and counted as income were collected. Some billed in prior fiscal periods and counted as income for those periods were collected in this period. And some billed in this period and counted as income were *not* collected. This line also reflects the fact that not all expenses on the income statement require cash. Depreciation is an example. Depreciation, by definition, is the decline in the value of an asset used in the production of income. As a refresher, assume that $10,000 worth of kitchen equipment is acquired, and that cash is paid for this equipment. The cash was spent today. The income statement will not recognize as an expense the total outlay of cash for the equipment. It will depreciate this asset (kitchen equipment) by systematically writing off its cost over the useful life of the equipment. This is consistent with the concept that not all expenses require expenditure of cash to be shown on the income statement. It also reconciles the practice whereby some items ultimately requiring cash are not treated as expenses for this fiscal period. For example, consider personnel pay for the last few days of December. Using the accrual method, the accountant would treat these unpaid wages and salaries as an expense of the fiscal year ending. But cash would be spent in the new fiscal year.

Refer now to the line, other sources. This section of the cash statement encompasses sources of cash apart from sales of food, expenses incurred in generating sales, and other normal business transactions. Here, as you will note, depreciation *is* shown as a source of cash, as is amortization and decrease in prepaid insurance. Other sources might also include cash generated from the sale of stock, the sale of equipment no longer needed, the sale of bonds, and cash generated from additional investment in the company by the owners.

The line, applications of cash, includes all uses and disbursements of cash resulting from other than normal operating transactions. In addition to those entries shown in Exhibit 11–1, purchase of land, buildings and equipment, retirement of stock, and investment of company funds in other enterprises would fit in this category.

The differential, then, between cash received from all sources and cash expen-

ABC Company

STATEMENT OF CHANGE IN

FINANCIAL POSITION

For Year Ending Dec. 31, 19xx

SOURCES OF CASH		
From Operations	$30,000	
From Other Sources		
Depreciation	4,000	
Amortization	2,000	
Decrease in prepaid insurance	2,000	
Total Sources		$38,000
APPLICATIONS OF CASH		
Withdrawal by owner	$28,000	
Reduction of current liabilities	1,000	
Purchase of furn. & fixtures	9,000	
Retirement of long-term debt	2,000	
Total Application		$40,000
NET DECREASE IN CASH		$ 2,000

EXHIBIT 11–1   A typical cash statement.

ditures for all but regular operations is the figure yielded by the cash statement, in our example a net decrease of $2,000.

Exhibit 11–2 (p. 135) is a *comparative balance sheet* of the same company covering a calendar year. It shows that cash was $10,000 as of January 1, and $8,000 as of December 31. (The cash statement, Exhibit 11–1, explains why cash has decreased by $2,000.)

Our example assumed a net income for the year of $30,000. This represents profit after expenses, and is a source of cash. Accumulated depreciation is shown to have increased from $6,000 to $10,000. This means that throughout the year the firm has, on its income statement, expensed $4,000 of depreciation. The firm did not pay out cash for this depreciation. Because depreciation was shown on the income statement as an expense (appropriately), because depreciation does not require cash, and because we started the cash statement with net income, it must be added back to net income.

Certain transactions have required the use of cash. Throughout the year the owner has withdrawn $28,000 for personal use. At the beginning of the year the firm had furniture and fixtures which cost $46,000. At the end of the year furniture and fixtures had a cost value of $55,000. Throughout the year management purchased $9,000 worth of furniture and fixtures requiring the use of cash. For this reason, the accountant shows these purchases as an application of cash.

At the beginning of the year debts classified as long-term debts were owed in the amount of $22,000. At the end of the year the firm had reduced the long-term notes payable to $20,000, thus retiring $2,000 of this debt. This retirement of long-term debt was an application of cash.

Throughout the year the company decreased the current asset titled prepaid insurance. Since the use of the insurance, which had expired, was shown on the income statement as an expense which decreased profit, and since the company did not pay for any insurance policies this year, the accountant has to add back the $2,000. During the year the company reduced current liabilities by $1,000, which caused the company to use up $1,000 of cash.

Since the firm had only $38,000 in sources of cash and a $40,000 outflow of cash, it had a net reduction in cash of $2,000. Exhibit 11–1, the cash statement, shows this $2,000 decrease. Exhibit 11–2, the comparative balance sheet, shows $10,000 cash as of the beginning of the year, and $8,000 cash as of the end of the year. Simple arithmetic shows that cash has decreased by $2,000, the same amount cash had decreased as shown in the cash statement.

Solvency and Cash Management

It is of course important that any company maintain solvency (the ability to pay debts as they mature). The cash statement helps management keep a close watch on solvency by showing changes in major accounts. Since solvency is so vital, every change in cash must be carefully analyzed. Management should also plan for future changes in the cash position. If a foodservice organization contemplates expanding present facilities by 50 percent, for example, it must ensure that sufficient cash is available to finance the expansion. It might be disastrous for a company if it ran out of cash in the middle of a major remodeling project and had to abandon it; such poor planning could hurt the company substantially and even force it to go out of business.

The prudent financial manager recognizes that mismanagement of cash can itself be extremely costly. Under certain conditions in the money market, management may enjoy the luxury of mismanaging cash, so to speak, because it is easy and relatively inexpensive to borrow it. At other times the cost of borrowing money may be drastically higher. When money is hard to get and interest rates are high, top management is more and more obligated to husband today's cash and plan the use of tomorrow's cash.

The cash statement will show management other pertinent facts necessary for effective cash management. It will show whether normal operations produce an inflow of cash into the company. It will show what unusual transactions have occurred that caused cash inflow. And it will show what financial transactions required the use of cash.

The *historical* cash statement shows what has happened to cash over the last fiscal period. It is extremely helpful also for the management team to prepare a *projected* cash statement. This may be shown for each month of the coming twelve-month period. By looking at this projection of monthly change in cash position, management can readily determine the estimated amount of cash it will need to borrow at any future time, and the amount of excess cash it is likely to have available for investment.

It is essential to know in advance the approximate amount of money that may be needed from the bank, and the expected duration of the loan. It is especially important to project the cash needs of the company in times of tight money. When money is more easily available, cash budgeting is less critical, but will still be a desirable and more orderly way to proceed. Since the banker is in many circumstances the financial right arm of management, it is advisable to show him that the business is well planned and efficiently run. The banker cannot help being impressed if during a routine visit to the bank, for example, the foodservice manager notifies him that in approximately six months the company will be needing $50,000 for 90 to 120 days. The banker would no doubt be substantially less impressed if he were confronted by a manager saying he needs $60,000 by tomorrow afternoon to meet the payroll.

Put excess cash to work. The company sometimes generates more cash than it can profitably use in normal operations. When this occurs management should put the excess cash to work in the most effective way. Several options are available. The money can be invested in stocks, bonds, commercial paper, certificates of deposit, federal bonds, or passbook savings at the local bank, and in other ways. The wise decision will depend on the amount of money, how long it will be available to earn a return, and a number of facts about the current money market. Assume that the company has $50,000 in the checking account and no immediate call upon it. Depositing this money in a savings account would yield a minimal return. For a better return on its money, let's say management elects to invest in 90-day certificates of deposit with the local bank. If the company were to cash these certificates be- fore the end of the 90-day period, it would be penalized by a loss of some of the interest. This is a simple example

ABC Company
COMPARATIVE BALANCE SHEET
For Year 19xx

	January 1		December 31	
Current Assets				
Cash	$10,000		$8,000	
Inventory	5,000		5,000	
Prepaid Insurance	3,000		1,000	
Total Current Assets		$18,000		$14,000
Fixed Assets				
Furniture & fixtures	46,000		55,000	
Less accum. depreciation	6,000		10,000	
		40,000		45,000
Leasehold improvements	26,000		26,000	
Less amortization	6,000		8,000	
		20,000		18,000
Total Fixed Assets		60,000		63,000
TOTAL ASSETS		$78,000		$77,000
Current Liabilities				
Current accounts pay.	10,000		10,000	
Other current liabilities	4,000		3,000	
		14,000		13,000
Long-Term Liabilities				
Notes Payable, Long-Term		22,000		20,000
TOTAL LIABILITIES		$36,000		$33,000
Capital		$42,000		$44,000
TOTAL LIABILITIES AND CAPITAL		$78,000		$77,000

EXHIBIT 11–2   A report showing the company's financial position at the beginning and end of the year.

illustrating the need to know the length of time the money can be spared for "work" outside the business. Many other factors will of course apply.

Financing the successful business requires a lot of thought, and not a little luck, in planning and budgeting for cash needs. In the absence of such foresight and good fortune, the comptroller (money manager) of the company might find, upon preparing a projected cost statement, that the company needs a substantial amount of money with no ready source of repayment. This means going to the bank for intermediate if not long-term financing, such as a mortgage loan on real estate, and these are extreme and costly financial undertakings. No matter how diligent and forehanded, the accountant cannot make the business succeed. But good accounts and timely statements can cushion the shock of bad business turns, and point the way to a smoother recovery.

SOURCES OF FUNDS

Stocks and bonds are the principal sources of long-term financing, and if we add retained earnings and franchise funding we complete the picture of sources open to the foodservice manager for obtaining necessary capital. We have given some attention to bank loans, credit buying and other forms of short-term financing, and will now focus on financing methods that reach beyond day-to-day operational requirements. We may logically apply the term *capital funding* to this longer-range financing since it involves money contributed by owners—either direct contributions in exchange for stock, or indirect contribu-

tions in the form of earnings reinvested in the company—and does belong in the capital column on the right-hand side of the big-T ledger.

Stocks

There are two general classes of capital stock—*common* and *preferred*. Many varieties exist within these classes, and their differences lie mainly in the rights of the holders with respect to control, income distribution and disposition of assets in the event of liquidation. The most basic of the two classes is *common stock*, the voting stock of the corporation. If only one class of stock is issued this stock is sometimes called capital stock. The holders of common stock are actually the owners of the company. As owners they are the entrepreneurs, with the greater stake and the greater risk in the operation. They have no special rights or privileges in case of liquidation and would be last on the list of those with claims on the assets of the company. On the other hand, there is no limit on the dividends that can be paid on common stock, since the holder shares in the growth and profit of the company. This of course makes common stock a good investment if the company has steady growth and good earnings.

Preferred stock, as the name indicates, is stock which has some preference over common stock. Dividends of a specified amount are paid on this stock and must be paid before dividends can be paid on common stock. Since the holders of preferred stock do not share in the total growth and profit of the company, its value rests on the ability of the company to meet its obligations and on the

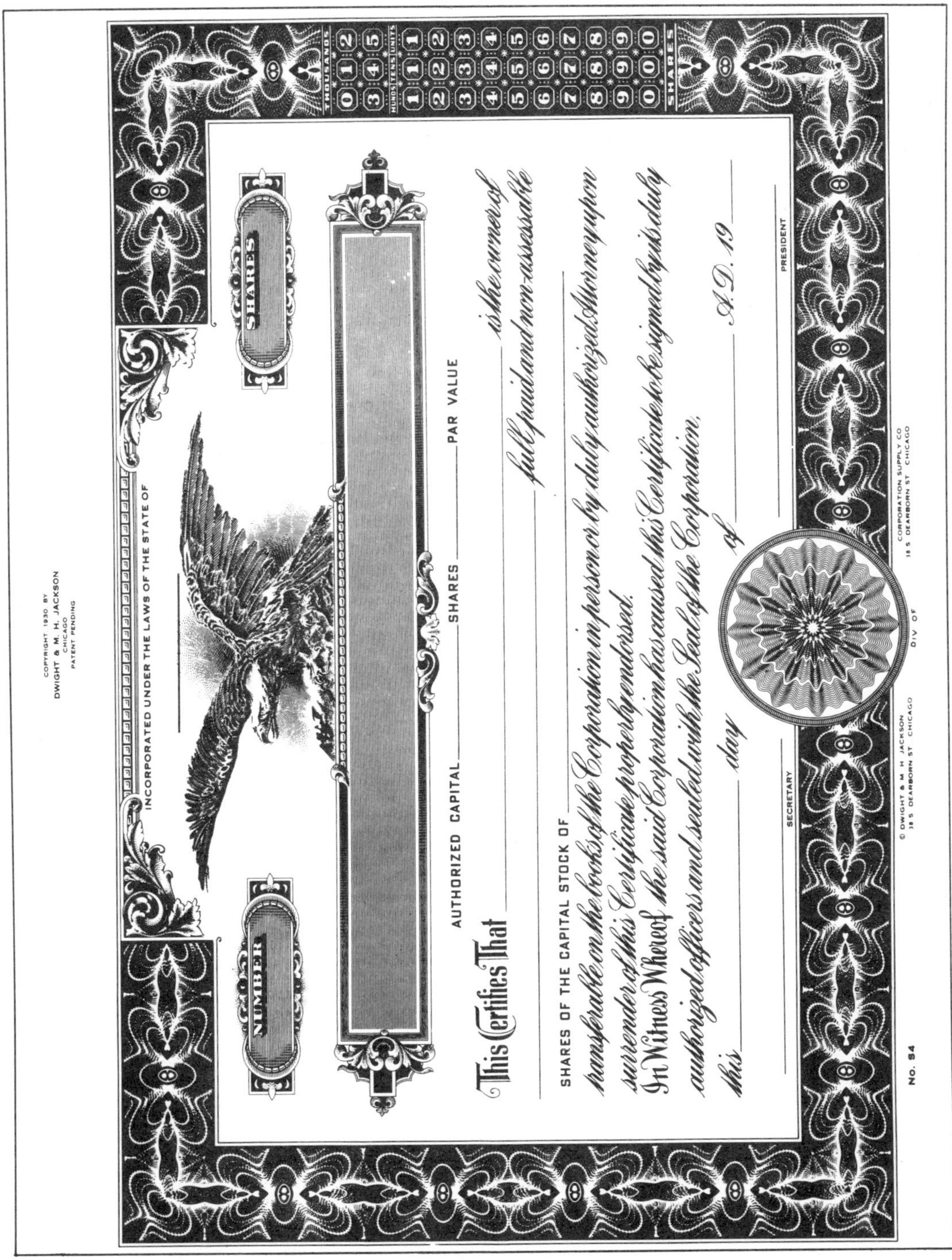
COPYRIGHT 1930 BY
DWIGHT & M. H. JACKSON
CHICAGO
PATENT PENDING

NUMBER

SHARES

INCORPORATED UNDER THE LAWS OF THE STATE OF

AUTHORIZED CAPITAL ____ SHARES ____ PAR VALUE

This Certifies That ____ is the owner of

____ full paid and non-assessable

SHARES OF THE CAPITAL STOCK OF ____

transferable on the books of the Corporation in person or by duly authorized Attorney upon surrender of this Certificate properly endorsed.

In Witness Whereof the said Corporation has caused this Certificate to be signed by its duly authorized officers and sealed with the Seal of the Corporation,

this ____ day of ____ A.D. 19

SECRETARY

PRESIDENT

NO. 54

© DWIGHT & M H JACKSON
18 S DEARBORN ST CHICAGO
DIV OF
CORPORATION SUPPLY CO
18 S DEARBORN ST CHICAGO

EXHIBIT 11–3 Standard form for a stock certificate. (Reverse side shown on next page.)

For Value Received, _____ hereby sell, assign and transfer unto _____ _____ Shares represented by the within Certificate, and do hereby irrevocably constitute and appoint _____ Attorney to transfer the said Shares on the books of the within named Corporation with full power of substitution in the premises.

Dated _____ 19 _____

In presence of

_____   _____

THIS SPACE IS NOT TO BE
COVERED IN ANY WAY

COPYRIGHT, 1920, BY
DWIGHT & M. H. JACKSON
CHICAGO
PATENT PENDING

(RESERVE THIS SPACE TO PASTE BACK CANCELLED STOCK CERTIFICATE)

(THIS SPACE RESERVED FOR ORIGINAL ISSUE REVENUE STAMPS)

Certificate No. ______ *For* ______ *Shares*

Dated ______ *19*__

Issued to ______

Received this Certificate ______ *19*__

Surrendered this Certificate ______ *19*__

IF NOT AN ORIGINAL ISSUE SHOW DETAILS OF TRANSFER BELOW

Transferred from	*Original Certificate No.*	*Original Certificate Date*	*No. of Orig'l. Shares*	*No. of Shrs. Transf'd*

IF THIS CERTIFICATE IS SURRENDERED FOR TRANSFER SHOW DETAILS

New Certificate Issued to	*No. of New Certificate*	*No. of Shares Transferred*

EXHIBIT 11–4 Stock certificate transfer record.

current value of money being used. In the case of "cumulative" preferred stock, if dividends are not paid in any year, they accumulate and must still be paid before any dividends on common stock. Preferred stock is purchased for stability and income. It raises money from investors who do not wish to participate in the company except as investors. It carries no specific time for redemption by the company. Preferred stock is secured by the good faith and success of the company. It does not provide as much security to the investor as bonds, but more than that provided by common stock.

Bonds

Bonds represent a kind of long-term financing that is usually a more difficult way of raising money than by either common or preferred stocks. Common stock offers the advantage of participation in the management, growth and profit of the company. Preferred stock provides for payment of a prescribed income percentage to the holder. Either can be purchased in small denominations and numbers of shares. Bonds are not usually as negotiable as stocks. They are customarily issued in units of $1,000 and sold in multiples of five. Bonds are often secured by designated assets of the business. They may, for example, be secured by a specific parcel of property owned by the company, and in this case operate as a lien against that property. Bonds carry a specified date for redemption. Failure to pay interest on bonds, or to be able to redeem them at the proper time, will cause the company serious financial problems that could lead to failure and liquidation.

Financing the business through issuance of stocks and bonds involves procedures controlled by law and must be authorized by the state in which the business is incorporated. This form of financing would not be used by a proprietorship or partnership. On the other hand, raising money through bank loans, mortgages, extension of credit by purveyors, and the sale of assets is common to all forms of business ownership.

Retained Earnings

Retained earnings are a significant source of capital, especially for growth companies. As indicated by the term, they represent earnings not distributed as dividends and not otherwise paid out to owners. Many companies distribute little of their profits, electing to use the money to foster growth. And stockholders who wish to see the company grow, and the value of their stock increase, find this policy agreeable. Exhibits 11–3 and 11–4 (pp. 137–139) show a typical stock certificate and the form used to transfer ownership of stock on corporation books.

The Franchise

In recent years many foodservice enterprises have financed their growth through the medium of franchise ownership and organization. The financing arrangement in franchise operations varies greatly. For a fee, and usually a substantial owner investment, the franchisor will furnish the operator advice and counsel and often a considerable measure of financial aid. The franchisor also furnishes technical services, which may include market research, lease negotiation, site evaluation, building plans and architectural services, training programs and advertising support.

The franchisee operates according to the agreement with the parent company, usually paying a fee based on gross sales. Depending upon the terms of the franchise, the operator may or may not be required to repay the franchisor's original investment. As can be seen, the arrangement may significantly increase the amount of capital available to the individual seeking to go into business, and provides the foodservice chain with a method of expansion that has built-in controls.

THE FEASIBILITY STUDY

A feasibility study may be characterized as "the look you take before you leap." Whether undertaken in a formal and elaborate way or not, a careful study will surely be made by any prudent person contemplating a major business venture. This should include a realistic appraisal of the individual's own goals and capabilities, as well as a market survey. The depth of the research will of course depend upon the nature and extent of the project. When substantial investments are proposed it is well to have the feasibility study conducted by a qualified professional. We incorporate this subject in our discussion of financing to emphasize that long-term financial commitments should never be made without careful consideration of all the factors involved.

With this in mind, let's review the elements of a typical feasibility study. A regional foodservice chain, we will assume, is considering opening a branch in a new, planned-development community. Here are some of the facts bearing upon the decisions of the planners:

- General description of the development: area, number of units, population, etc.
- Income of residents
- Traffic flow
- Convention facilities
- Number of tourists
- Number and character of competitive operations
- Estimated cost and profitability
- Labor market analysis
- The menu and style of service
- Menu pricing
- Anticipated average check
- Sanitation requirements
- Financing
- Laws regulating sale of liquor
- Entertainment

These factors are listed more or less at random. An almost limitless number of other considerations will arise for the circumspect planner. And, indeed, virtually any factor, however remote it may seem, that can be measured with reasonable accuracy, should be considered.

It is difficult for the businessman, as well as the tiger, to check his spring in mid-air.

SUMMARY

Management must know when and how much money the company will need at any one time. It is essential for management to anticipate the cash requirements of the company so it can plan the sources from which it will be able to acquire the money needed. It is also essential to anticipate excess cash so that its investment can be planned.

The statement of changes in financial position (cash statement) is a generally required financial statement which should be prepared when the accountant prepares other financial reports. This statement shows sources of cash, the applications of cash and the net increase or decrease in cash for the fiscal period.

Customary means of financing a corporation include the sale of common stock, preferred stock and bonds. Common stock represents ownership in the business and is rewarded by the growth and prosperity of the company. Preferred stock receives a set return on investment and its dividends take precedence over dividends paid on common stock. Also, its claim on assets in the event of liquidation of the business precedes that of common stock. Bonds represent the most difficult form of fund-raising for the corporation and the most secure form of investment for the investor.

Corporations, partnerships and proprietorships all raise capital through bank loans, mortgages and extension of credit by purveyors.

The franchise form of business organization has enjoyed extensive growth in the foodservice industry in recent times. Since the franchisor usually provides the franchisee with many services in addition to financial assistance, franchises are especially interesting to the independent business man or woman who may have difficulty obtaining these services on their own.

The feasibility study, an elaborate "trial run" on paper, is an essential prerequisite to any business undertaking. With it, the planners seek to project every foreseeable condition and event in order to determine whether to invest their money and, if so, how much and in what direction.

STUDY QUESTIONS

1. What does the statement of changes in financial position (cash statement) show management?

2. Why should management know if additional cash is required or if excess cash is going to be generated by the company's operation?

3. Depreciation is an expense on the income statement that does not require the outlay of cash. Explain.

4. Explain how a company could have a cash-shortage problem but be making substantial profits.

5. Explain how a company could be showing substantial losses but have excess cash on hand.

CHAPTER 12

MANAGEMENT OF WORKING CAPITAL

About 'fluid' assets other than cash

PURPOSE

To examine methods of controlling the flow of working capital in managing a business enterprise, with emphasis on short-term capital funding in the foodservice establishment.

CONTENT

Working Capital Defined: Current Assets Less
   Current Liabilities

Short-Term vs. Long-Term Funding

Liquidity

Cash Cycle in a Foodservice

Sources of Working Capital
   Inventory turnover
   Additional investment
   Addition to long-term debt

Applications of Working Capital

THE NEED FOR MANAGEMENT to be well informed on its cash position and continuously on the alert to make the best possible use of cash was pointed out in Chapter 11. Our discussion of the cash statement showed how many options there are in administering cash assets.

Here we consider operating funds in the broader context of *working capital,* which is defined as *the amount remaining when we deduct current liabilities from current assets.* For the foodservice manager this basically means:

Working Capital
= (Cash + Inventory)
— (Accounts Payable + Current Debts)

The cash statement limits itself to a picture of cash and changes in the cash account. Working capital views all current assets and all current liabilities, not just cash. Stated more simply:

Working Capital
= Current Assets — Current Liabilities

From this equation it is evident that the management of working capital involves more than reacting to the company's cash position, because cash is just one component of current assets. A company's cash position is sometimes put in the form of a ratio. As will be remembered from Chapter 5, this is the *quick ratio,* which measures the company's ability to pay short-term debts as they mature and involves in its numerator current assets

less inventory. Usually the test used is the *current ratio*—the relation between all current assets and current liabilities—which measures the company's ability to pay all its bills. Management does not make absolute decisions on the basis of these measuring sticks, but considers a number of other factors, such as the effect of long-term obligations on the present position.

Before examining working capital more closely, let us review what is meant by current assets and current liabilities.

Current assets: Those assets which are cash, will be converted into cash within the year, or will be consumed within the year. Examples include change fund, checking account, accounts receivable, inventories, and prepaid expenses such as insurance premiums.

Current liabilities: Those obligations which will have to be paid within the year. Examples are accounts payable, taxes payable, tax money withheld from employee paychecks, accrued payroll and other accrued expenses.

In a typical situation a foodservice organization may have current assets of $30,000 and current liabilities of $20,000. Its working capital would be the difference: $10,000.

The following examples analyze some typical transactions and show what effect each has on working capital.

1. The business purchases $1,000 of inventory for cash. The effect on working capital is no change. This can be seen by noting that the transaction in-

creased inventories and decreased cash. The current assets of cash were decreased by $1,000, and the current assets of inventory were increased by $1,000. The net change to current assets was zero. Current liabilities did not change. The net change to working capital was zero.

2. The business purchases $5,000 worth of equipment with cash. What is the effect upon working capital? The effect on current assets is a reduction of the current asset cash. The effect on current liabilities is no change. Since the transaction reduced current assets by $5,000 without reducing current liabilities, working capital has been decreased by $5,000.

3. A creditor is paid $2,000. The effect on working capital is zero. The current asset cash has been reduced by $2,000. The action also reduced current liabilities—accounts payable—by $2,000. Since both current assets and current liabilities have been reduced by equal amounts, the result is that working capital has not changed.

Because working capital is the difference between current assets and current liabilities, increasing current assets and current liabilities by equal amounts will produce no change in working capital. Decreasing current assets and current liabilities by equal amounts likewise produces no change in working capital.

Knowing the amount of current assets in relation to its current liabilities, management can evaluate the firm's ability to pay current debts as they become due. The firm's ability to pay is known among accountants and business people as its *liquidity* position. If the foodservice has a large amount of current assets and very few current liabilities, the firm is considered to be in a "good" liquidity position. It would mean the company might even lose money for a period of time and still be in a position to pay its debts as they become due. On the other hand, if the foodservice has few current assets and a great many current liabilities, the firm will most likely have difficulty meeting its obligations. This could be true even though the company's financial statements showed a profitable operation.

Long-term funds are a very important part of any firm's financing. Looking at the average foodservice operation one will find that most of the required financing is for long-term or long-lived assets. The financing of these assets is done primarily through long-term funds and, as a general rule, involves a larger dollar volume than that considered as current working capital. Land, buildings and equipment are, under normal conditions, financed with long-term arrangements: mortgages, bonds, stocks, and other forms of owner investment. Each method of financing will involve the operator with a different set of considerations.

It would be extremely difficult for a new business to pay off the mortgage on the building or a note on major equipment in one or two years. These are long-lived assets which are expected to pay for themselves and provide the firm a return on its investment throughout their life. For this reason it is customary in purchases or investments of this type to extend them over a period of years, letting the asset pay its own way. Very rarely would a new company be in a position to pay cash for such basic assets. Careful study should precede the decision to assume a long-lived obligation. It is necessary for management to assure itself, from the information available, that the asset will generate sufficient income to pay for itself and to return a fair profit to the owners. In view of this, and since the obligation will remain in effect for many years with, most likely, few opportunities to "manage" it, a highly circumspect approach is advisable.

The mortgage is a very common method of acquiring assets. Having decided that the asset is essential to the company, and once the transaction is completed, management can turn its efforts to other things. In a dynamic money market timing is of course important if management is to succeed in obtaining the mortgage funds at the lowest possible cost (interest). Whatever the cost of financing, management must anticipate the payment of fixed principal and interest in the operation of the business. As the mortgage loan matures it may be refinanced, since the firm is acquiring a free and clear asset.

Bonds are a less common means of acquiring assets. Bonds may raise funds for general purposes (cash) or for the purchase of a particular asset. They are obligations maturing at a specified date at a specified rate of interest. Management must determine whether the cost of issuing the bonds and the interest to be paid are within the company's capability to generate income. A bond issue represents a major, long-term financial commitment, and once undertaken is difficult and expensive to change.

Preferred stock is often quite an attractive way for the money-manager to provide the firm with necessary funds. Although a dividend on his investment is guaranteed to the stockholder when earnings warrant it, there is no specific redemption date, which means the stock will not be redeemed except at the convenience of the company. Preferred stock carries many guarantees which are enticements to the prospective purchaser, and one of its most attractive features is the security it offers. An issue of 5,000 shares of $100 preferred stock, for example, is a financial covenant both sides may normally expect to last for a period of years.

Management should occasionally review its position with respect to long-term financing. Even though it is relatively expensive to retire bonds, under some conditions it may be advantageous for the company to do so. Because of the dynamic nature of the business world the money-manager must be alert to changing conditions, to be sure that previous decisions are still in the best interest of the company.

Since short-term financial needs fluctuate greatly, it follows that a substantial amount of management's time is spent in this area. The volume of business in any given week in a foodservice operation may be extremely heavy. Meeting such demand in an efficient way requires good planning and inventory control if sufficient food and supplies are to be on hand. It also means forehandedness in cash control since cash is often demanded on delivery of foodservice merchandise. Generally speaking, however, management of short-term capital is less critical than in some other industries, since foodservice is primarily a cash business; that is, it receives cash as soon as the customer eats the meal. As an illustration, consider the flow of short-term working capital in a manufacturing operation and compare it to that of a foodservice operation. We will assume that, to manufacture a particular product, the plant carries an inventory of raw materials sufficient for one-month's production. Manufacturing the product takes one-week's time, after which it is stored for an average of three weeks in the warehouse before being shipped to the customer. After the item is shipped, the average customer takes the maximum credit time and does not pay for it until thirty days have elapsed. From the time the raw material was received until the finished product was paid for, at least eight weeks have elapsed.

Cash Cycle in a Foodservice

In a foodservice operation there is a substantially shorter period of time between purchase of raw material and receipt of cash. The operator may purchase food supplies this week and convert those purchases into cash this week or next week. Many items purchased never go into storage, but are received, placed into production and served the same day. Since the foodservice business is primarily a cash business, it follows that the cash *could* be returned the same day it was used to purchase the raw materials. From the example cited it is evident that the problem of working capital and its management is less critical for the average foodservice than for a typical manufacturing firm. Just because the problem is less critical, however, is not to say it is any less important in the management of the company. Often the responsibility of having sufficient cash available to buy necessary merchandise

and supplies weighs heavily on the operator.

Now let us take a closer look at the cycle of converting purchases of materials into cash. As indicated, the main accounting function involved is that of controlling the time merchandise is held in the storage or production area. Since most items must move quickly out of the production area, the inventory control and, perhaps, accounts receivable are areas vital to the cash cycle. Although a foodservice operation must acquire certain foods and keep them in inventory at all times so that customers may be served upon ordering, the conversion cycle from inventory to cash is relatively short. Food purchased this week will probably be processed and sold this week or next.

Credit

Although foodservice transactions are primarily for cash, banquets and certain other accounts will confront the operator with credit sales, and at times accounts receivable may call for more than passing attention. Credit cards speed the collection process, but there may still be an undesirable lag between servicing the customer and collecting for the service.

Since the company and its accounting system are mainly geared for cash operations, the manager must watch the amount of credit business, the reliability of its creditors, and the length of time money is withheld. In times of tight money and high interest rates the cost of extending credit may not be inconsiderable. And the very nature of the business transaction—the product is consumed on the premises—makes credit sales a greater risk. Moreover, this added risk makes a restaurant's accounts receivable less valuable at the bank, should the business need to raise cash on this asset. Management should also be conscious of the "aging" factor: accounts usually become increasingly difficult to collect as they become older.

Credit Purchases. Since the company has been organized to make a profit for its owners, management must recognize that paying for materials on delivery may not be as advantageous to the company as paying for them in 30 days. Money in hand can be used to earn interest or profits. If management yields up its cash before it has to, it relinquishes control over the money and the opportunity to realize interest on it. As a general practice management should therefore postpone paying a bill until it is due. In short, it is good policy to work for liberalized credit terms and husband the company's assets.

Credit Standing. Managers of a business should of course recognize that it is necessary to live up to the credit terms to which they are committed. If the company has purchased food and agreed to pay for these purchases in five days, management has an obligation to pay the suppliers on or before the fifth day. Not living up to such a commitment may drastically reduce the ability of the company to get credit in the future. But there are ways open to the resourceful buyer, who can get the purveyor to sell the merchandise for the same price, but allow the foodservice 30 days, rather than 5 days, in which to pay. This permits the company's cash to work for an additional 25 days.

The kind of credit arrangement described above can be beneficial to the supplier as well as to the foodservice operator. The supplier may induce the foodservice operator to pay early by offering a discount for cash. The terms for cash are often payment by the tenth of the month, instead of the last day of the month following the invoice date. Under these conditions, the purchaser must weigh the discount against the value of interest on his money. The following example will illustrate.

The manager is negotiating with a supplier to furnish a shipment of food for $1,000. The supplier has proposed these terms: At the end of the thirtieth day the foodservice is obligated to pay the supplier $1,000; or, if the account is paid within 10 days after receipt of the merchandise, the supplier will allow a two percent discount. (The supplier has determined that use of the money is worth more to him than the two percent allowed.) The foodservice manager must now decide how valuable the use of the money is to his operation. If he waits until the thirtieth, the foodservice must issue a check for $1,000, but if he elects to pay in 10 days, it must write a check for only $980. The manager would reduce the cost of this food by paying the invoice 20 days early. If he carefully analyzes the facts, he will have no trouble in deciding which alternative to choose.

Solution: A two percent reduction in cost may not sound like a substantial amount and, by itself, a $20 reduction on a $1,000 invoice may not appear to be substantial. This two percent, however, becomes very meaningful when it is recognized that the foodservice may be purchasing such quantities every week.

Purchasing $1,000 worth of food each week and earning the two percent discount on each of the 52 purchases will amount to an annual saving to the firm of $1,040. In this example management would be wise to pay for the material on or before the tenth day and take the two percent discount. If the company does not have the cash to pay the supplier on the tenth day, it should consider going to the bank and borrowing the money in order to take advantage of the discount. It could well be that the cost of the borrowed money would be significantly less than the discount savings throughout the year.

SOURCES OF WORKING CAPITAL

Working capital is derived from inventory turnover, additional investment, and addition to long-term debt.

Inventory turnover—converting inventory into sales revenue—is the primary source of working capital. Each time we serve a customer and collect cash we produce more working capital. In some cases management will find it advantageous to sell its products and services on account. Here inventory is converted into cash when the payment is received. It is important to collect these accounts as soon as possible in order to have use of the cash.

Additional investment is not a regular source of working capital for most companies. When the business is first organized, owners usually invest sufficient funds to support its operation and do not expect to commit additional money. As a matter of fact, owners normally expect to remove cash from the business as their share of the earnings.

Owners may put up additional working capital for a major expansion project or when the company has lost money for a period of time, and they can expect, with additional financing, to recover the loss and eventually have a profitable operation.

Addition to long-term debt is by no means an everyday occurrence, as mentioned in our discussion of financing methods. This source of capital usually involves large amounts of money and extensive commitments.

On some occasions it will be found that working capital can be obtained by selling certain assets of the company, such as unused land and surplus equipment.

APPLICATIONS OF WORKING CAPITAL

Working capital in the form of cash is required for the following kinds of transactions:

> Payment of expenses
> Retirement of debt
> Purchase of assets
> Payout of earnings

A major demand on working capital is generated by the requirement to pay expenses incurred. As each invoice comes due, the firm must pay the suppliers for items purchased. Each week the firm must pay employees their wages. Each month the firm must pay utility bills, advertising bills, and other expenses. Liquid working capital is needed for discharging these obligations.

Having borrowed money in the past, the foodservice will have to retire this debt in the future. Having acquired a building and financed its purchase through a mortgage, each month a check must be written to the mortgage-holder.

The purchase of additional assets also may require the use of liquid working capital. When it purchases new kitchen equipment, for instance, the firm reduces its working capital.

Since the owners have invested money in the business, they expect a share of the earnings at regular intervals. Corporations distribute profits in the form of dividends to their stockholders. If the operation is a small proprietorship or partnership, the owners will withdraw, probably on a weekly basis, a share of the profits.

SUMMARY

Working capital is the amount remaining when *current liabilities* are deducted from *current assets*. Current assets are assets in the form of cash, assets that will be converted into cash within the year, or assets to be consumed within the year. Current liabilities are obligations that have to be paid within the year.

Management of working capital is an extremely important function of the foodservice operator. Since decisions relative to capital invested in long-term projects exist over long periods of time, little of management's current time is devoted to long-term financing. Management is mostly involved with short-term financing because of wide fluctuations in working capital. Cash is a liquid asset which management should endeavor to keep at work. Money collected today is more valuable than money which will be collected in a year.

Since there are so many demands on working capital, great care should be taken in a periodic analysis of the working capital position. The analysis should include present position and trends.

STUDY QUESTIONS

1. Define the following: (1) Working capital; (2) current assets; (3) current liabilities.
2. Why must managers spend a lot of time managing working capital?
3. Name and explain two methods of long-term financing.
4. Name and explain two methods of short-term financing.
5. Why is it good business to observe credit terms strictly? Discuss from two standpoints of the creditor.

CHAPTER 13

INFORMATION FOR DECISION-MAKING

'Guesstimates' are not good enough

PURPOSE

To examine the operational areas which require decision-making in a food-service enterprise; and to review the sources of information, internal and external, available to management in reaching decisions.

CONTENT

Management Information from Within
    Sales and marketing
    Food preparation and service
    Finance and accounting
    Personnel
    Management information systems
    Planning and forecasting

External Sources of Information
    Government
    Industry associations
    Academic institutions
    Trade press

A man's wisdom is most conspicuous where he is able to distinguish among dangers and make choice of the least.—Machiavelli

THIS STATEMENT by the noted Italian political philosopher, intended for the guidance of rulers, applies equally to the manager of a modern business operation. When the benefits and penalties of a management decision are obvious, the decision is also obvious. But often decision-making involves the weighing of indistinct advantages and disadvantages that must be traded off, one against the other. The wisest choice may often be the least disadvantageous course of action selected from several undesirable alternatives.

The foodservice industry is highly competitive. And in this competitive environment the manager who regularly makes sound decisions based on the best information available is soon separated from the manager who makes "gut" decisions based on limited understanding and information. To reach good decisions the successful manager requests advice from the accountant and refers to special sources of information that throw light on specific problems. In this chapter we will see how financial advice can be helpful in various areas of management, and examine the information sources available to the foodservice manager which make for better decision-making.

MANAGEMENT INFORMATION FROM WITHIN

Except for the specialist in a large establishment, a foodservice manager is called upon to make decisions affecting a variety of operations: sales and marketing, food preparation and service, finance and accounting, personnel, management information systems and planning and forecasting. We will look briefly at each of these areas and suggest the kinds of information a manager needs in reaching sound decisions. Much of this information can be provided by an accountant even though it may reach beyond the data normally presented in financial statements.

Sales and Marketing

As a basis for menu planning, purchasing, and profit analysis, the foodservice operator should prepare forecasts of current, intermediate and long-range customer demand both for the number of covers and for specific menu items. These forecasts are useful to the manager in decisions relating to staffing, food and equipment purchasing, and overhead costs. Sales forecasts are also useful in evaluating the performance of the operation as a whole.

Early in the game the manager must decide how varied the menu will be. He will want to know how simplification or extension of the menu will affect sales and profitability. In planning the menu the manager will need to know the actual and the estimated costs of each item on the menu, and the extent to which sales of each item contribute to the overall profit of the operation.

Menu decisions should be based on adequate historical information and careful experimentation. Accordingly, systems must be established for accumulating useful data. The manager will need to ensure that the burden of these systems does not outweigh the benefits they yield, and this is often no easy matter. Wearing his management consultant hat, the accountant is usually prepared to give advice on the development of such systems.

In marketing and sales promotion the manager also faces decisions on how compensation of service personnel can best contribute to sales. Does the compensation system encourage service personnel to promote sales by providing efficient and prompt service? Would the payment of commissions to service personnel be beneficial? An experienced financial consultant can provide significant inputs for solution of this problem.

Food Preparation and Service

The foodservice manager regularly makes decisions intended to promote the efficiency of operations. Full utilization of staff is likely to be the key to increased efficiency. Elimination of waiting time offers the most obvious, and probably the readiest, means at hand in improving staff productivity. Operating skills will come with doing, but supervisors can directly influence the event by minimizing time spent by the kitchen staff waiting for raw food to be moved into the work area from storage, time spent by the kitchen staff waiting for food process and cooking operations to be completed, time spent by the cleanup staff waiting for areas to be cleared, and time spent by the table service staff waiting for food to be prepared. Improved staff utiliza-

tion can be achieved through improved sequencing of operations and better traffic control in the routing of personnel and materials. These are tactical controls that are clearly in the hands of the manager, while the "dollar" aspects of these problems are proper concerns of the financial assistant.

The foodservice manager must consistently be concerned with quality control, determining standards for the quality of meals served and the quality of service. Controlling quality will yield benefits in innumerable ways, some measurable immediately in terms of fewer customer complaints and food returns, and some measured tomorrow in the form of repeat business built on reputation. In deciding on standards, the manager should consider historical data accumulated by the accounting department showing the proportion of wastage to sales volume, and relating staffing levels to sales.

Information developed by the purchasing department will help the manager decide whether he is deriving a full measure of value from vendors and from his purchasing procedures. Often the manager must decide whether it is more economical to purchase prepared foods or to prepare food in house. Actual product and labor cost data developed within the operation provide the best guidance.

For both kitchen and service operations, the manager must decide upon the degree of automation that will offer the greatest return on investment. Realistic costing of existing operations and careful estimates of the impact of additional equipment are logical starting places for such decision-making. The purchase of equipment and other additions to fixed assets should pay their own way in increased efficiency or increased sales.

Finance and Accounting

The restaurant accounting system should be designed to provide management with ready information on which to make planning and control decisions. This means that the information produced by the accounting system must be accurate, timely and significant, and be directed to those who make the operating decisions. If it is all these things, the next obvious "must" is that it be *used* by managers in their decisions.

To produce usable information, the accounting system must be carefully adapted to the specific establishment. Accounting routines which generate financial statements should be closely tied in with cost accounting mechanisms that provide operational data. Cost accounting should in turn supply detailed information supporting food and labor cost analyses. Through "exception" reporting, the cost accountant aids the manager in his decision-making by highlighting costs that are out of line or operating ratios that are not consistent with prior experience.

Budgeting simplifies management decision-making by providing a standard against which to measure financial performance. Since restaurant operations often fail because of inadequate cash flow, cash budgets are exceptionally important in restaurant operations. Changes in operations or business conditions should lead promptly to budget revisions, thus providing managers with standards that give effect to the changed circumstances.

The manager of a restaurant operation frequently makes decisions relating to the investment of capital in equipment and facilities. These decisions should be anticipated, guided by budget considerations and economically justified. Usually the accountant is prepared to help the manager in these decisions and in identifying sources of capital. A foodservice manager is often confronted with critical problems concerning the balance between debt and equity capital, when additional capital funds must be raised.

Personnel

Effective managers continuously review their staffing levels to determine whether the operation is over- or understaffed for optimum profitability. Decisions in this area can be helped by studying the historical relationship between labor costs and sales volume for his own operation and similar statistics for the industry. Wage and salary levels should be compared to local standards in making policy decisions. These comparisons are only valuable insofar as they are based on similar job descriptions of the responsibilities and duties for all major positions in the organization. These position descriptions are also useful in developing a manpower budget. For a large restaurant operation, the manager's judgments on staffing matters should be guided by a personnel budget in the same way investment and expenditure decisions are guided by a financial budget.

Management Information Systems

It is a continuing responsibility of management to evaluate the system which provides the information it requires for decision-making. Management must determine whether the output of management information systems, including accounting and cost control mechanisms, is geared to the needs of management. The information produced by the system should in all respects *facilitate* control. It is possible that the system is producing too many reports, or reports that are too complicated in their presentation of information. The reports required by management should be reviewed periodically to eliminate information not required and to revise information provided so that it accords with the changing needs of management.

The reports should emphasize management by exception, permitting managers to concentrate their energy on areas requiring attention. When a manager decides to investigate a particular problem area, the information system should provide supporting details to assist in that inquiry. In short, management must remain alert to its own needs for pertinent, timely and factual information.

Planning and Forecasting

The planning and forecasting functions of management are vital to the decision-making process. Profit objectives for the foodservice operation and the plans for achieving them should be generally understood by all who participate in managerial decisions. Regular reviews should be conducted by the foodservice manager on the progress made toward the company's profit goals and the contributions made by each department in the operation. Plans and forecasts are largely based on prior sales information. This information includes customer acceptance of specific entrée items as well as overall sales volume for periods of operation. Industry-wide forecasts should also be considered in developing long-range plans to guide future decision-making.

EXTERNAL SOURCES OF INFORMATION

We have described the sources of information within a foodservice operation that are valuable to the manager in making decisions. The success or failure of a foodservice is also affected by conditions outside the operation. Changes in food prices, economic conditions in the industry and throughout the nation, population growth and movement—all are influential factors. The manager must be as aware as possible of the external sources affecting his business and have access to adequate information regarding them.

The federal government collects and disseminates statistical information on the foodservice industry and on related industries such as food processors, packers and distributors. These reports indicate trends in food costs and preferences and provide various other data of interest to the typical foodservice operation. Publications of the U.S. Department of Commerce and the U.S. Department of Agriculture may be especially helpful. Listings of relevant publications from the Government Printing Office, Washington, D.C., are provided at no charge.

Local chambers of commerce and travel and tourist bureaus are valuable sources of information on local or community conditions. Information provided by these agencies may include an economic profile of the community, data on population trends and projections, tax rates, numbers of tourists and how much they spend, new construction, the labor market, and other factors influencing local business enterprises. Because utility companies must make long-range plans in servicing local communities, they are sources of information on population trends and areas of prospective commercial and residential development.

Trade associations representing foodservice companies as well as other industry associations are valuable sources of information. Often these associations foster research within their industries and publish the results. Regional and national meetings conducted by these groups include seminars and other educational activities of value to the foodservice operator. Trade shows exhibiting new equipment and food products help keep the foodservice manager abreast of changes in food technology and marketing.

The National Institute for the Foodservice Industry (NIFI), sponsor of this textbook, is an excellent source of educational materials and information on the industry. Originally an affiliate of the National Restaurant Association, the Institute is now an independent foundation supported by the foodservice industry. In cooperation with the national and state associations, with government agencies, and with other educational institutions, it administers courses in management education, conducts a national scholarship program, and engages in foodservice education and manpower research. NIFI's publications and programs are all directed to the specific needs of restaurant and institutional foodservice managers.

In recent years many new books have been published on the subject of the management and operation of foodservice establishments. Many of these publications are available from technical publishers, trade associations and libraries. The libraries of educational institutions with foodservice management curricula are a further source of educational materials on the industry, including audio-visual aids useful in employee training.

A number of national magazines are exclusively oriented to foodservice operations. These include *Institutions/ Volume Feeding, Hospitality,* and *Food Service Management.* Some of the publications are highly specialized, such as *Drive-In* and *Fast Foods.* In order to keep current in an industry that is rapidly evolving, every foodservice manager should regularly read at least the periodical with greatest significance for his own operation.

SUMMARY

The successful foodservice manager is, among other things, an information consumer. Decisions on how to operate the business should be based on the most timely, reliable and pertinent information available. This requires information both from within the establishment and from the wider social and economic environment in which it operates.

We have seen that much of the data needed for effective control of foodservice operations must originate at the operating point, and that, although this feedback goes beyond the data represented in routine financial statements, the accountant can provide valuable assistance in collecting and analyzing it.

We have identified the operational areas requiring scrutiny—sales and marketing, food preparation and service, finance and accounting, personnel, management information systems and planning and forecasting—and reviewed the data-keeping and analysis procedures appropriate to each.

The external sources of information available to the foodservice manager include the federal government, chambers of commerce, travel and tourist bureaus, trade associations, educational institutions, libraries, and periodicals directed specifically to foodservice subjects and events. All of these sources provide information of practical value in the management of a modern foodservice enterprise. The successful manager takes full advantage of them.

STUDY QUESTIONS

1. Assume that you plan to increase sales by means of an advertising campaign.
   a. What market information would you need?
   b. What information would you require from your own accounting and control systems?
   c. What external sources should you consult for the information you require?

2. Your maitre d'hotel has requested a 10 percent raise in salary. He is rather insistent. Your decision should be based on the best possible information.
   a. What data would you expect to obtain from within your own organization?
   b. What information would you seek from external sources?

3. Based on an industry-wide study, you find that your food costs are 10 percent higher than the national average. You wish to determine whether this difference exists because of your food preparation practices, your purchasing procedures, or because of local market conditions.
   a. What information would you need in order to reach a meaningful conclusion in this matter?
   b. What information sources should you consult?

4. In what area of your operations is it most important to have current information?

5. What problems are you likely to face if the information you receive on your operations is not current?

6. Assume that your inventory records were not maintained properly over a period of two months.
   a. How would a problem of this kind most likely be discovered?
   b. In what way would you expect this record-keeping error to affect your purchasing and menu-planning decisions?

PART FIVE

THE FINAL ANALYSIS:
ACCOUNTING FOR PROFIT

CHAPTER 14

FOOD AND BEVERAGE COST CONTROL

How costs can be assets in fact as well as in name

IN RECENT YEARS the foodservice industry has experienced a problem common to many sectors of the American economy: an upward cost trend that exceeds the growth rate of sales revenues. The result is a profit squeeze. The percentage of profits has dwindled for each additional dollar of sales. Our inflationary economy has focused attention on the techniques of cost control as a means of preserving reasonable profit margins in the foodservice industry.

Let's take a closer look at the significance of cost control. Assume that a foodservice operator makes $7,500 profit on $100,000 of sales. Viewed another way, $13,333 of sales produces $1,000 of profit. Accordingly, $1,000 of savings through cost control in this operation is equivalent in value to sales of $13,333. Obviously, cost control is one of the quickest routes to greater profitability.

In this chapter you will learn how cost control can help to combat the effects of the inflationary spiral and how cost control can help the foodservice operator to maintain a competitive price structure.

A food and beverage cost control system, like other management and accounting systems, must be adapted to the particular needs of the organization. The benefits of a cost control system may be lost through the use of excessively complicated procedures where simple ones would be appropriate.

In a small foodservice operation, the functions of food receiving, storage and issue may very well be grouped together.

In a larger operation, these functions would be separated, with specific cost control procedures applying to each function. If menus are complicated, then more cost control effort must be devoted to the development of purchasing specifications than is the case when menus consist of only a few items.

FOOD COST CONTROL

For purposes of food cost control, a foodservice operation may be divided into nine different functional areas. Each of these areas will have an impact on the overall financial performance of the foodservice operation. Persons responsible for each of these functional areas exercise some degree of financial control. These functional areas include: (1) management; (2) menu planning; (3) purchasing; (4) receiving; (5) storing; (6) issue; (7) preparation; (8) sales; and (9) accounting (see Exhibit 14–1). In the following pages we will see how control exercised through these functional areas contributes to the overall goal of cost savings.

Management

Management is, of course, responsible for the overall conduct of the business. In carrying out this responsibility, management determines policies and objectives, develops systems of control and surveillance, interprets reports and takes corrective action on the basis of those reports. If functional areas are to mesh effectively, management policies must be stated clearly and be understood by all concerned. The successful operation of a business depends on this common understanding of policies and objectives.

Two of the tools available to management in securing a common understanding of policies and objectives are the organization chart and budget. The organization chart, along with a defini-

tion of the duties of each position in the organization, will help achieve control through a common understanding of responsibilities. When each member of the organization has a clear understanding of the financial responsibility for which he or she will be accountable, there is little possibility that these financial responsibilities will be neglected. A real-

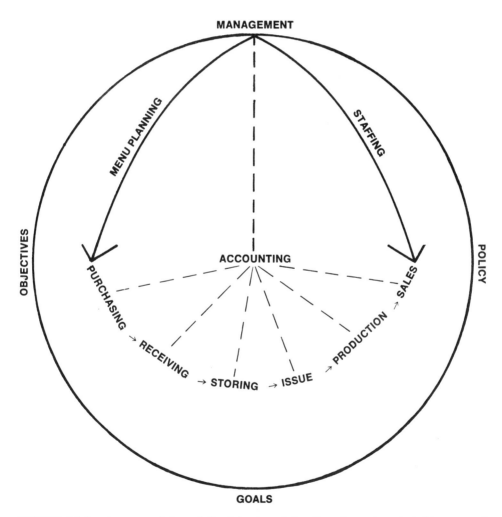

EXHIBIT 14–1   A representation of the interplay of functions in cost control. Management policy both conditions and shapes the complex activities involved.

istic budget will promote a general understanding of expected financial performance. Through comparison of actual costs and budgeted costs, financial performance can be evaluated on a continuing basis. When financial performance is thus found to be unsatisfactory, management can examine the causes and take action. When financial performance is better than anticipated by the budget, management can learn how similar performance can be achieved in the future.

By demonstrating its own cost-consciousness, management encourages similar behavior throughout the organization. When management insists upon adherence to cost control procedures, and judges performance by well-derived standards, a general awareness of cost control is created that leads to improved performance in all departments.

Menu Planning

Through the menu, the menu planner should be able to predict costs with a high degree of reliability. In arriving at costs for the menu, the menu planner will need to use standard portions based on standard recipes, and will need to know the current prices being paid for products, the results of kitchen tests for edible portions and customer acceptance of different recipes. Sales histories of specific recipes should be developed through daily cost records, and these sales histories should provide guidance to the menu planner in selecting recipes for the current menu.

The type of clientele being served is another important consideration in menu planning, significantly influencing the quality of food and beverages being purchased, methods of preparation, portion size and pricing. The menu for a foodservice operation serving a group of retirees in Florida would obviously be very different from a menu for a first-rate hotel in Manhattan. Menu planning for a foodservice operation in a college dormitory likewise would differ markedly from that for a hospital.

There are significant cost benefits in keeping a menu as simple as possible, considering the clientele being served. A simple menu reduces the skill level required of employees. A simplified menu reduces the workload on the kitchen staff and tends to increase the efficiency of their work. In addition, reducing the number of items on the menu simplifies the task of the purchasing agent, receiving clerk and storeroom personnel.

Standardizing the menu for a definite period of time permits greater detail in menu planning. A cyclic menu, one which repeats every 28 days, for example, allows the planner to take advantage of local market conditions and to obtain discounts for quantity purchases. This cycle must of course be adjusted for seasonal influences on local market conditions and seasonal influences on clientele tastes. The menu planning must be flexible enough to accommodate foods associated with holidays, sporting events or other special occasions.

Planned use of leftovers is necessary in minimizing menu costs. This will allow savings through quantity discounts in purchasing and, in effect, means more efficient use of the kitchen staff. Fresh food stock on hand as well as the existing stock of leftovers should always be reviewed as inputs to the menu planning process.

Pricing is a critical step in preparing a menu. There must be a calculated relationship between prices and the popularity of the food items offered. Both the competitive situation and the customer's willingness to pay must be considered in determining prices. Obviously, a foodservice operation with excessively high prices will lose patronage. Conversely, profit margins will diminish if prices are set too low.

There is a simple process for pricing items once the desired percentage of markup for the item is known. The percentage markup deducted from 100 equals the percentage food cost of the selling price. Note the following equation for determining selling price:

$$\frac{\text{Actual unit cost of the item}}{\text{Percentage food cost of selling price}}$$
$$= \text{Selling price}$$

Assuming our actual cost for an item is 80¢ and the percentage of food cost of selling price is 40 percent, we can make the following substitution:

$$\frac{\$.80}{.40} = \$2$$

As you can see, with a 60 percent markup, a 40 percent food cost, and an actual food cost of 80¢, our selling price is $2.

In determining the selling price of items on the menu, the percentage markup is not usually applied in a uniform manner. Allowances must be made for customer preferences for menu items and customer price acceptance. Accordingly, some items may be priced above the desired markup, and others may be priced below it. In general, the pricing should produce an overall sales figure which reflects the desired percentage markup.

A record of selling costs and actual costs for each menu item should be maintained. The best way to do this is to take a copy of the menu and record the entrée portion costs on the menu itself next to the selling cost of the entrée. This record of sales price and actual cost for entrée portions should be reviewed regularly so that sales price adjustments can be made to assure that the overall sales markup is achieved. As costs change due to local market conditions, regular prices may be adjusted. A menu example, including the selling price and the estimated cost per portion, is shown in Exhibit 14–2.

Purchasing

Purchasing by written specification is an all-important food and beverage cost control procedure. Detailed descriptions of the items we intend to purchase are provided to vendors along with purchase orders or invitations for bids. Copies of specifications will also be required for the head of the kitchen staff and receiving clerks. Written specifications are necessary so that the same product is purchased regardless of who places the order, and to assure that none of the requirements for the food or beverage item are forgotten when the order is communicated to the vendor.

Specifications usually include the following information:

1. Trade name or common name of item.
2. Amount being purchased and unit of purchase.
3. Grade or brand name.
4. Container size or number of packages.
5. Additional information necessary to identify the product as to grade or other quality.

Here are some sample specifications:

Item: Boneless strip sirloin steak, 8–10 lbs., cut 2″ above eye on flank end, cut below 12th and 13th ribs. All aged surfaces trimmed off. Aged approximately 3 weeks.

Item: Tomato juice, canned. California pack. US Grade A (fancy), 12 cases. Cases packed 12/46 oz. cans to case. Cans lined with acid-resistant enamel.

All purchasing must be done on the basis of known future need. Nothing should be purchased that does not appear on the current or planned menus. Purchased items that do not appear on the menu cannot be sold and their purchase will result in spoilage, overproduction or pilferage. Quantity buying must be done on the basis of consumption and the buyer must be guided by adequate records. These records should include the sales history of menu items (the record of customer demand), information on edible portions in relationship to purchased quantities, and copies of current and previous menus. In addition, a record of local quantity food prices should be maintained.

Generally the purchaser will gain a price advantage by soliciting competitive bids. Of course, vendors must bid on the basis of written specifications so there is legitimate price competition in providing the same product. Bids should be solicited from no fewer than three different vendors. In the case of very large orders, or orders involving foods of exceptionally high cost, even more than three bids may be appropriate. Bid in-

The Supper Club
STANDARD MENU AND ESTIMATED PORTION COST

Appetizers

Shrimp Cup	$1.00
Baked Onion Soup	.50
Clams on Half Shell	.75
Garde Manger Salad	

	Selling Price	Estimated Cost per Portion
Strip Steak	$4.50	$1.20
Veal à la Viennoise	3.75	1.00
Shrimp Newburg	3.95	1.00
Brook Trout Sauté	3.50	.90
Prime Rib of Beef	4.25	1.00
Lobster Tail	4.75	1.20
Delmonico Steak	4.25	1.05
Beef Stroganoff	4.50	1.15
Cheese Cake	.50	
Austrian Strudel	.39	
Parfait	.50	
Beverage	.50	

All meals include complimentary house wine.

EXHIBIT 14–2   An example of the relation between food costs and menu pricing.

formation is recorded on market quotation sheets or call sheets. An example of such a sheet is shown in Exhibit 14–3.

Quality specification should be a stated policy. For example, management may specify that only prime grades of meat be purchased for roasts and steaks, and that choice grades be purchased for stews and soups.

In assuring the appropriate quality of the foods purchased, both raw food and canned food tests should be made occasionally to determine if the foods purchased satisfy type specifications and the overall quality standards of the food-service operation. Checks on the quality and edible portions of meat cuts are particularly important. Kitchen tests should also consider the relative merits of purchasing pre-prepared foods, oven-ready, fresh, frozen, or table-ready foods.

Receiving

A foodservice grossing $300,000 spends between $100,000 and $150,000 on food purchases. Too many operations entrust the receiving of these valuable purchases to anyone near the unloading or storage area when the shipment arrives. When responsibility for receiving is not fixed, and procedures are not systematized, careless losses, failure to assure quality and quantity, and pilferage may cost the foodservice more than its net profit each year. Properly designed and enforced controls over receiving will ensure management that it is receiving a dollar's worth of quantity and quality for every dollar spent.

Responsibility for the receiving function should be assigned to a specific individual. In a small operation, this in-dividual may well have additional duties. Insofar as possible, the person responsible should not be involved in food purchasing or preparation. The receiving clerk should be provided with the same specifications sent to the vendor with the purchase order or bid invitation. Obviously the receiving clerk must be able to understand the specifications and to use them in evaluating the quality and quantity of goods received.

It is management's responsibility to set up receiving procedures and to ensure that they are being carried out. The hours established for receiving should not interfere with the work of the kitchen staff or other functions of the organization. Deliveries should be permitted only within specified hours to prevent disruptive movements of goods in and out of the storage area.

In order to work efficiently, the receiving clerk should have a few simple items of equipment. These include an accurate scale, a crowbar and hammer, wire cutters and a special knife for opening cardboard boxes. The receiving clerk should have ample work area. If the foodservice uses a lot of ground meat, the receiving clerk should be equipped with a device for measuring the percentage of fat in the ground meat. The receiving clerk counts, weighs or measures every incoming item, inspects all merchandise and checks the incoming merchandise against written specifications for grade and quality. In addition, all incoming meat is weighed and tagged.

If the delivery is acceptable, the receiving clerk signs for all incoming goods, and keeps a record describing the item. As goods are received, he completes a daily receiving report. This form

MARKET QUOTATION SHEET

Date _____

ON HAND	ITEM	WANTED QUOTATIONS				ON HAND	ITEM	WANTED QUOTATIONS			
	BAKERY						Baking Powder				
	Apricot Glaze						Almond Paste				
	Apple Filling						Food Color				
	Cherry Filling						Almonds				
	Pineapple Filling						Fudge Base				
	Lekvar Filling						Malt				
	Holland Rusk						Piping Jel				
	Crackers, Bulk						M. F. B.				
	Crackers, Indv.										
	Almonds										
	Pancake Mix										
	Muffin Mix										
	Blueberry C. Mix										
	Poundcake Mix										
	Corn Meal										
	Honey										
	Lemon Powder										
	Vanilla Extract										
	Lemon Extract										
	Rum Extract										

EXHIBIT 14-3 A standard form for recording competitive bids.

is kept in duplicate, one copy remaining with the receiving clerk and the original going to the accounting department. Receiving slips are attached to the original copy returned to the accounting department. An example of this report is shown in Exhibit 14–4.

Truck drivers for the vendor making the delivery should remain in the receiving area until the products have been properly received and signed for. If the products are unacceptable, they can be returned to the driver or the driver can call his supervisor for further instructions.

Too often unsatisfactory merchandise is received and accepted without proper credit for defective products. It is very easy to overlook products that do not entirely satisfy specifications after the driver, who is a representative of the vendor, has left the premises and is no longer available. The receiving clerk must be prepared to notify the purchasing agent or the head of the cooking staff if items do not fully satisfy specifications. If items are accepted even though they do not fully satisfy specifications, a request-for-credit form must be completed by the receiving clerk. Copies of the

---

The Supper Club
DAILY RECEIVING REPORT

Date _____

ITEM	PURVEYOR	P.O.#	AMOUNT
1			
2			
3			

Total _____

Signed: _____
Receiving Clerk

EXHIBIT 14–4

request for credit are sent to the vendor and to the individual responsible for the purchasing function. A typical request for credit is shown in Exhibit 14–5.

Storage

Well-designed storage areas contribute to cost control by preserving inventories and limiting access to authorized persons only. Obviously, food and beverages must be stored at the proper temperatures in clean, pest-free areas. Poor storage conditions can result in significant loss of value through deterioration and spoilage.

If possible, responsibility for storage areas should be centered in one individual. Management policy should limit the hours in which storage areas are open. Only authorized personnel in the process of placing goods in storage or issuing and receiving goods should be permitted in the storage area. Access should be closely controlled. Keys to the area should be in the custody of designated personnel at all times.

Inventories held in storage represent a significant investment of the company's assets. Although the monetary value of foods and beverages in storage will be clear to management, employees may not

---

The Supper Club
REQUEST FOR CREDIT

Date _____

ITEM	PURVEYOR	P.O.#	AMOUNT

Reason for Request of credit:

Signed: _____
                Receiving Clerk

EXHIBIT 14–5

The Supper Club
SUPPLIES REQUISITION

Following supplies requested for issue:

Unit Qty or Size	Article	Brand	ck	Price Per	Total

Ordered by: _____

Issued by: _____

Date _____ 19 _____

EXHIBIT 14–6

look at a pound of butter or a can of tuna in the same light. Employees who would not steal from the cash register may see nothing wrong in taking an item from storage now and then. But this is pilferage, and a practice management must not tolerate.

Foods and beverages in the storage area should be considered "money in the bank" and treated accordingly. Anything taken from the storage area should be drawn by means of a requisition slip, and these requisition slips should be periodically reconciled with inventory records. See example in Exhibit 14–6.

In general, there are two methods of maintaining inventory records for the control of foods and beverages in storage. A monthly count can be taken of all goods held in storage, and the count should represent the balance of goods received into storage less issues from storage. This form of inventory control and record-keeping is appropriate for small storage operations and for goods with a low unit value.

When monthly accounting for stored goods is necessary, a perpetual inventory is maintained. A perpetual inventory requires a card for each type of goods in storage. All additions to stock are entered on the card and likewise all withdrawals are recorded. As a result, the balance shown on the card for a particular type of goods in storage should indicate the actual quantities on hand at that time. A perpetual inventory card is illustrated in Exhibit 14–7.

INVENTORY

Page _____

Sheet No. _____   Priced by _____

Called by _____   Extended by _____

Entered by _____   Examined by _____

Ck	Qty.	Description	Unit Price	No. Rec'd or Issued	Balance

Amount Fwd.

EXHIBIT 14–7

These two inventory record systems may be combined. For example, storage items of high value, such as meats, might be recorded on a perpetual inventory card, and inventory records on low-value, bulk items such as potatoes and flour would be maintained through a monthly count. When the monthly count is used, the individuals doing the counting should be completely independent of the persons responsible for the storage function.

Issue

The issue of goods from the storage area is basically controlled through the use of requisition slips. Only a few kitchen personnel—for large operations the heads of different departments—should be authorized to sign requisition slips. No goods whatsoever should be issued from the storage area without a requisition slip bearing an authorized signature. If issuance of goods from the storage area is limited to specified hours, department heads can plan their withdrawals and reduce record-keeping.

In order to create cost-consciousness among kitchen personnel, it is desirable for the storekeeper to price out requisition slips and enter the total value of the goods withdrawn on each slip. Stamping the cost on top of a box or carton when it arrives (as is done in a supermarket) saves the storekeeper time when he prices out a requisition slip. Again, stamping the purchase price on food products issued makes the kitchen staff aware of the value of the products they are handling and increases their awareness of costs. As a check on both the

kitchen and the storage function, the total value of requisitions from the storeroom can be compared to food costs as a percentage of daily sales.

Preparation

No competitive foodservice operation can afford less than the maximum percentage edible yield from raw food products entering the kitchen. Through a knowledge of standard percentage edible portions, the kitchen supervisor can exert some control over wastage during initial food preparation. However, there may be considerable variation in the quality of raw food products of the same type and grade. To determine the actual maximum percentage yield for the food products purchased, the kitchen supervisor should conduct frequent food preparation tests. By closely supervising kitchen personnel, the supervisor can assure that the maximum yield, determined through his own tests, is actually produced by the kitchen staff. Supervisory effort in training the kitchen staff will also pay off. Proper techniques in cutting, slicing, boning, trimming and peeling will minimize wastage.

The use of standardized recipes is also a valuable cost control technique. Through standardized recipes, costs and raw food quantities can be more reliably estimated. Standardized recipes help assure that correct cooking temperatures, cooking times and food quantities will be used, reducing spoilage and preventing dryness and shrinking of foods. Shrinkage represents a loss in final edible portions, and dryness may seriously impair the flavor of foods. The standard

THE SUPPER CLUB
MENU

Appetizers

Seafood Cocktail   1.00   Baked Onion Soup   .50
Clams on the Half Shell   .75

*   *   *

Salad

The Supper Club Salad Tray with Choice of
Dressings

*   *   *

Entree

Grilled N.Y. Strip Steak	~~IIII~~ ~~IIII~~ ~~IIII~~ ~~IIII~~ ~~IIII~~ III	4.50	12%
Veal Viennoise	~~IIII~~ ~~IIII~~ ~~IIII~~ III	3.75	8%
Brook Trout Saute	~~IIII~~ IIII	3.50	4%
Prime Rib of Beef	~~IIII~~ ~~IIII~~ ~~IIII~~ ~~IIII~~ ~~IIII~~ ~~IIII~~ ~~IIII~~ ~~IIII~~ ~~IIII~~ ~~IIII~~ ~~IIII~~ III	4.25	25%
Lobster Tail	~~IIII~~ ~~IIII~~ ~~IIII~~ ~~IIII~~ ~~IIII~~	4.75	10%
Delmonico Steak	~~IIII~~ ~~IIII~~ ~~IIII~~ ~~IIII~~ ~~IIII~~ ~~IIII~~	4.25	13%
Beef Stroganoff	~~IIII~~ ~~IIII~~ ~~IIII~~ ~~IIII~~ ~~IIII~~ ~~IIII~~ ~~IIII~~ ~~IIII~~ ~~IIII~~ ~~IIII~~ I	4.50	17%
Shrimp Newberg	~~IIII~~ ~~IIII~~ ~~IIII~~ ~~IIII~~ ~~IIII~~ I	3.95	11%

240 PORTIONS   *100 %*

Vegetable

Choice of Potato:
Baked Potato w/Sour Cream & Chives,
Chopped Crisp Bacon
Au Gratin
Parsley Buttered
Carrots Vichy, Parsley   Buttered Green Beans

*   *   *

Beverage

Choice of:
Milk, Coffee, Tea, or Iced Tea
Dinner Breads and Butter

*   *   *

Desserts

Cheese Cake   .50   Austrian Strudel   .30
Parfait   .50

EXHIBIT 14–8   Scorekeeping for the "calculated menu mix." A copy of the customer menu is used
to keep tab of entrée acceptance.

recipes used should result from deliberate experimentation and tests under the direction of highly qualified personnel. Once standardized, recipes should be closely followed in order to produce the greatest customer satisfaction and least wastage during the cooking process.

Carefully selecting kitchen equipment reduces the fixed costs of a foodservice operation. Where menus are simplified as much as possible considering the tastes of clientele, kitchen equipment can be selected for the greatest efficiency. Where menus are highly varied, more versatile kitchen equipment may be required. Careful planning in selecting kitchen equipment according to anticipated menus and customer tastes will produce cost savings through reduced investment, more efficient preparation and reduced labor costs, and minimum food waste and spoilage.

Standard portions represent a further and extremely important cost control technique. The quantities of foods purchased should be determined through estimates of the numbers of standardized portions to be served. After the food is prepared, carefully selected kitchen and table service utensils help assure that meals are served in standardized portions. Serving-spoons and spatulas in the kitchen, and cups, bowls, glasses and plates used in table service should all be calibrated to standard portions. As an additional control over prepared food leaving the kitchen, the kitchen may retain a duplicate guest check. Food quantities used by the kitchen can then be compared to standard portions served by the kitchen, determining quantity losses in food preparation and service.

Historical sales records of particular meals served will guide the restaurant manager in cutting production costs. Failure to use this guidance may result in overproduction and excessive leftovers. Cooking in small amounts often results in more flavorful meals and will also combat overproduction, but labor costs have to be considered. When it is apparent that overproduction will occur, plans should be made immediately for the prompt use of leftovers in order to prevent loss through spoilage.

Sales

Sales records, if maintained in sufficient detail, contain some important messages for the foodservice operator. They will suggest ways of increasing sales through increased customer satisfaction and they will suggest ways of increasing profits through foodservice efficiency and cost control techniques. In evaluating menu acceptance by clientele, it is not enough to know which entrées are most popular. The foodservice manager should know the relative acceptance of all entrées on the menu. This data can be accumulated easily and simply by reviewing the meal checks for a specific menu item and entering the number sold on a copy of the menu. The percentage of total portions sold is then calculated for each entrée. This procedure has been used on the supper club menu shown in Exhibit 14–8.

A brief inspection of the menu in Exhibit 14–8 suggests that the next time we present this menu, we should probably be prepared to serve 60 portions of prime ribs of beef and only six portions of brook trout sautée. Indeed, considering the low customer acceptance of the brook trout, we would probably be justified in experimenting with a different entrée in the hope of winning greater customer acceptance.

By tabulating entrée sales on menus, as shown in Exhibit 14–8, for a period of several weeks, we can prepare an analysis of entrée sales as shown in Exhibit 14–9.

This analysis of portions sold can serve as a practical basis for quantity food purchases, resulting in significant quantity discounts. By averaging our sales of a particular entrée over a week or more, as shown in this analysis, we have a more reliable guide to food purchasing and menu planning than the results of sales for a single menu would provide. The kind of analysis shown in Exhibit 14–9 is also helpful in cycle menu planning.

In order to increase the efficiency of kitchen operations, it would be helpful to know the peak service periods for each mealtime. We can use this information to plan the staffing and hours of work of both kitchen and table service personnel. A knowledge of the time of peak demand during meal hours will help us control food preparation with the goal of improved food quality and service. To determine the time of peak customer service, we could prepare a summary similar to the one shown in Exhibit 14–10. This summary is prepared by entering the time on the guest check and then tabulating the results.

Records similar to those shown in Exhibit 14–11 and 14–12 can be developed as weekly and long-range guides for menu planning, food purchasing and staffing.

The Supper Club
ANALYSIS OF ENTREE SALES

	Portion Size	Week A		Week B		Combined	
		Amount	Ratio	Amount	Ratio	Amount	Ratio
Strip Steak	12 oz	168	12%	198	11%	366	11%
Veal à la Viennoise (2)	8 oz	112	8	182	10	294	9
Shrimp Newburg	8 oz	154	11	217	12	371	12
Brook Trout	12 oz	56	4	70	4	126	4
Prime Rib (1)(2)	10 oz	343	25	413	23	756	24
Lobster Tails	2-4 oz	147	10	161	9	308	10
Delmonico Steak	10 oz	182	13	252	14	434	13
Beef Stroganoff (2)	8 oz	238	17	307	17	545	17
		1,400	100%	1,800	100%	3,200	100%

(1) 14 cuts/22# rib.
(2) Prepared in advance.

EXHIBIT 14–9   A portions-sold tabulation to guide menu planners.

The Supper Club
NUMBER OF CUSTOMERS SERVED PER HOUR

Total covers per night	180	270	360	450
5:00– 6:00 P.M.	40	60	80	100
6:00– 7:00 P.M.	50	75	100	125
7:00– 8:00 P.M.	30	45	60	75
8:00– 9:00 P.M.	30	45	60	75
9:00–10:00 P.M.	20	30	40	50
10:00–11:00 P.M.	10	15	20	25

EXHIBIT 14–10   A summary showing day and hour of peak service, which can be used to guide production and staffing.

The Supper Club
NUMBER OF MEALS SERVED DAILY AND WEEKLY

September 19xx

	Week Number			
	1	2	3	4
Monday	193	223	240	226
Tuesday	240	218	216	231
Wednesday	195	219	229	189
Thursday	200	217	207	236
Friday	357	347	307	342
Saturday	355	361	393	364
Totals	1,540	1,585	1,592	1,588

EXHIBIT 14–11   A customer traffic count for days of the week.

The Supper Club NUMBER OF MEALS SERVED WEEKLY (by month)		
	Prior Year	Current Year
January	1,300	1,430
February	1,340	1,460
March	1,320	1,420
April	1,343	1,470
May	1,370	1,500
June	1,450	1,620
July	1,490	1,560
August	1,520	1,500
September	1,540	1,580
October	1,510	—
November	1,460	—
December	1,390	—

EXHIBIT 14–12   A count of customers by month for two successive years.

Exhibit 14–11 indicates the variance in covers served over the week during a particular month. Exhibit 14–12 indicates the average number of meals served per week during each month of the year.

Records should show employee meals served as well as those served to guests. Purchase, preparation and service records cannot be balanced unless the number and type of employee meals is known. As an additional control measure, specific employee menus and employee eating hours should be established. Most foodservices cannot afford employees who eat prime roast beef or lobster indiscriminately.

The Accounting Role

The demands on the accounting function are nowhere more stringent than in controlling food and beverage costs. Through the use of guest checks, cash register readings and storeroom issue slips, the accounting department makes a daily audit of sales. By reconciling food purchases with standard portions sold, accounting can assist management in monitoring food wastage and loss. By comparing current costs of food purchases with historical costs of food purchases, accounting personnel can highlight food costs that are significantly out of line. Regular balancing of these records obviously serves to help control costs.

BEVERAGE CONTROL

Laws governing the sale of beer, wine and liquor vary from state to state. Some states have local option laws. These allow governmental bodies within the state to exert local control over the sale of alcoholic beverages. In addition, the federal government has taxing and licensing authority over the sale of alcoholic beverages in interstate commerce. As a result, a foodservice establishment offering alcoholic beverages faces loss of license, fines and penalties if it is not in compliance with a complex body of law. The manager must have a thorough knowledge of applicable local, state and federal regulations and adhere to them strictly in order to remain in business.

Beverages require the same kind of controls as those required for food, but because of the nature and value of alcoholic beverages, controls must be tighter and more closely supervised. Since the sale of alcoholic beverages is closely supervised by governmental agencies, purchasing forms and other accounting records are often specified as well as methods for keeping track of sales. These

strictures limit the action of the operator but serve to emphasize the value placed on alcoholic beverages and the necessity of guarding against theft or misuse.

Authority for the purchase of alcoholic beverages should be reserved to the manager, purchasing agent or other responsible representative of the management. Usually, beers and wines will not need to be as closely controlled as liquors. Orders for beer and wine may be left to the bartender or bar manager. When beverages are received they should be carefully checked against the requisition forms. Cases should be opened and inspected for quantity and breakage. If merchandise is purchased by brand, the receiving clerk must check to see that the brands ordered are actually received, since different brands of alcoholic liquors vary greatly in price. Wine and liquor deliveries should be inspected by the receiving clerk to ensure that tax stamps are intact and properly affixed to the bottles.

Security of Liquor Stocks

To summarize, a high degree of security is required in the storage of alcoholic beverages because of their greater value. Only authorized persons should enter storage areas and keys should never be handed to unauthorized persons in order to move beverages from the storage area into service areas. Consistent security requires that proper inventories be maintained for all bottled goods and that spot checks of inventory be made periodically. Wine storage takes more care than is given other alcoholic beverages.

The wine cellar should be a room with temperature, ventilation and humidity control to prevent deterioration or spoilage. Wines can be very expensive and some vintages may be held in storage for long periods of time.

A control system is necessary for every bar operation regardless of the size of the bar. With automatic dispensing machines, which meter and mix drinks at the push of a button, this control is greatly facilitated. But even in establishments which use this equipment certain drinks are made by hand, introducing the need for other kinds of control. Pouring spouts and other measuring devices simplify portion control.

Operational Controls

A simple way to account for the amount of liquor sold is to check the issue of liquor to the bar against average sales. Additional control may be achieved by maintaining a fixed bar stock. The bartender reorders every day to replenish the fixed stock. This reorder, offset by an ounce inventory of open bottles on the bar, represents the liquor sold.

Strict portion controls as well as inventory checks are required to guard against losses, whether from carelessness, inefficiency and waste or from deliberate fraud. In dispensing liquor there are two fraudulent maneuvers to which management must be especially alert: (1) the bartender goes into business for himself by bringing liquor in and selling it over the bar; and (2) the bartender waters the drinks.

In the first instance, the bartender is selling his own liquor and pocketing the money. He is using the foodservice operation's equipment, glasses, mixes and clientele in his low-overhead operation. In the second instance, by getting two or three more ounces out of each bottle, the bartender can pocket the collections for these drinks.

The practice of watering the drinks can be frustrated, in part, through the use of a cashier. The bartender provides a bar bill or guest check to the patron who in turn pays the cashier. An audit of the liquor checks indicates the amount of liquor used and this amount can be balanced with actual bar inventories. If bar checks are not used in conjunction with guest checks for service of liquor on the floor, control may be established by providing each waiter or waitress with a cash fund. Serving personnel purchase liquors from the bar by using this cash fund or "bank." The amount expended by each server should equal the total for liquor on his or her guest checks.

SUMMARY

We have seen that specific food cost control measures are required for each functional area of a foodservice operation, as shown in the table on the opposite page.

Beverage control requires strict compliance with local and federal law. Extremely tight storage and inventory controls are required. Special security measures are needed to protect against fraudulent maneuvers and pilferage.

FUNCTIONAL AREA	BASIC COST CONTROL MEASURES
Management	Clear definition of responsibilities, budgeting, cost consciousness.
Menu planning	Standardized and cycle menus, records of cost per portion, and selling costs.
Purchasing	Use of specifications, competitive bidding, tests for quality and yield.
Receiving	Assignment of specific responsibility, inspection for quality and quantity, use of receiving reports, and requests for credit.
Storage	Limitation of access, appropriate inventory methods, use of requisition slips.
Issue	Balancing requisition slips with inventory.
Preparation	Staff training, standard recipes, standard portions, and tests for yield.
Sales	Complete records of entrées sold and covers served per hour as guides to menu planning, purchasing and staffing.
Accounting	Audit of sales, reconciling of food purchases and food sales, and balancing of purchasing, receiving, inventory and issue records.

STUDY QUESTIONS

1. Describe how management uses organization charts and the budget in exercising control over costs.

2. Discuss in about 100 words the role of menu planning in cost control.

3. Name four standard elements of a purchase specification and explain how purchasing functions contribute to cost savings in a foodservice.

4. As the commissary manager of a large restaurant you are outlining receiving, storage and issuing functions for personnel in your department. Describe the record-keeping procedures you would place in effect for maximum savings with minimum paperwork.

5. What do you see as the most significant economies to be realized from using standard recipes?

6. How would you go about organizing a sales analysis program best calculated to optimize sales and costs? Consider this problem from the standpoint of data-keeping, menu analysis, and customer traffic studies.

7. Aside from the legal aspects, what overriding consideration sets alcoholic beverage control apart in the management of foodservice establishments?

8. Recapitulate by functional area the kinds of accounting records and cross-checks maintained in controlling foodservice costs, naming at least six documents (sheets, slips, tabs, etc.) used in the system.

CHAPTER 15

LABOR COST CONTROL

Hard data tempered with some human engineering

PURPOSE

To consider ways in which management can most effectively extend its control over labor costs through systematic recruitment, training and use of personnel, recognizing that these measures require not only objective data analysis, but full appreciation of the human factors of leadership, loyalty and morale.

CONTENT

Management Responsibilities
    Policy-making
    Job analysis, description and specification
    Recruiting and selection of employees
    Orientation and training
    Counseling, career ladders and performance appraisals
    Staffing and scheduling
    Forecasting personnel requirements
    Record-keeping: The accounting input

Production Controls
    Menu planning
    Purchasing
    Service
    Clientele
    Hours of operation
    Design of facilities

THE COST OF LABOR in a foodservice operation is one of its two major expenses. It may be less than, equal to, or more than the cost of food, depending on the type of operation. It is a cost over which management has an element of control. Personnel policies, the layout of facilities, size and type of menu, hours of operation, style of service, clientele—numerous factors influence the quantity of labor to be recruited and the sources which must be explored to obtain it. In the following pages we will examine some of the principal ways in which management seeks to counter expense for wages with higher productivity and thereby improve its labor-cost position.

PERSONNEL POLICY

It is management's responsibility to establish personnel policy, which essentially has to do with finding the right people—the "round peg to fit the round hole"—and motivating them to produce at their maximum efficiency. Personnel policy is a broad term and embraces all the relationships that develop between management and the individual employees and, also, the relationships that develop among individuals in the organization. Effective personnel administration requires:

—Determination of employee classifications.
—Determination of the number of individuals to be employed within each classification.

—Recruitment of personnel.
—Analyzing, describing and writing specifications for each position.
—Personnel assignment and work scheduling.
—Development of employee training programs.
—Determining methods of appraising individual performance.
—Providing career ladders.
—Providing for employee counseling and the airing of grievances.

Classification and scheduling are mechanical. Other aspects of personnel administration involve a broad management approach which is more social in nature.

Job Analysis, Description and Specification

The first requirement in personnel procurement is to describe the job. And a job must be analyzed to be described. To analyze, according to the dictionary, means "to separate the whole into its parts or elements." So, when we analyze a position we separate the total position into various functions and skills. Unless we are aware of the various duties of a position it is impossible to describe it in sufficient detail to determine the qualifications necessary, in an employee, to fill that position. This analysis cannot be done hurriedly or in a haphazard manner. It requires time and should be done by someone having technical knowledge of the process. The worker

184

should be interviewed along with the supervisor of that position and others having first-hand knowledge of the work involved. The person analyzing the position should know: (a) the skills required of the worker performing the task and the manner in which it should be accomplished; (b) why the task is performed; (c) when the task should be performed; and (d) how to describe these requirements in clear, meaningful language. An outline of the position description should be prepared so that every detail is covered.

Using the job analysis, a description of the job may now be made in which the qualifications needed by the individual filling the position can be itemized, and the recruiter will know exactly what he is looking for when any position in the organization needs to be filled. The possibility of finding a person who will adequately fill the position, and who will stay with it and be enthusiastic, is tremendously improved by this method.

Recruiting and Selection

There is no one source from which all employees can be drawn. Recruiting must be done on the basis of the job to be filled. Since all jobs do not require the same amount of education, ability, or physical strength or other qualifications, the foodservice employer looks to various media for sources of qualified personnel. Newspapers, schools, churches, social service groups, employment agencies and other employees may all be of assistance. The degree of skill or education required for the position will, in some measure, indicate the procurement medium to be used. The foregoing sources would probably supply the operator with the bulk of his personnel needs. When the need arises for an employee of greater skill or education, the employer might turn to the two- or four-year colleges and technical institutes—schools specializing in teaching foodservice management and commercial food preparation—and he might advertise in trade and association publications and in financial periodicals.

Selection should be based on as many applicants as possible. This breadth of choice will depend on general business conditions and the availability of labor. In any case, careful selection will pay off in the long run. An individual lacking native ability or educational background for a job will probably not last long, finding the job too difficult. An overqualified person may, on the other hand, leave the job because it does not challenge his or her best abilities. Either of these risks can be minimized by good recruiting techniques. The application form itself must be broad enough in scope, and specific enough in describing the job, to elicit sufficient information from the applicant. The rest is up to the effectiveness of the interview and the judgment of the recruiter.

Employee Orientation and Training

Too often an individual is painstakingly hired and then given an insufficient introduction to the job, to fellow employees, and to the company. Making new employees feel at home in their new surroundings and as quickly as possible making them working members of the team will encourage feelings of loyalty and keep them in the job. At this time the newcomer can be introduced to company policy, and learn something of the background and goals of the company. The new employee should also be made aware of rules and regulations all staff members are expected to observe.

A well-conceived and well-executed training policy will help reduce turnover, improve efficiency and contribute to employee morale. Training should be continuous and can be used as a communication system by management to reach all employees. A trained employee will reduce costs by working with greater efficiency, will boost sales by producing a better product, and will help create a happy atmosphere that will be inviting to the trade.

Counseling, Career Ladders and Performance Appraisals

Providing the employee with someone to talk to, whether it be a professional counselor or the immediate supervisor, about problems both at home and at work, will help put the worker at ease and provide a sense of security. Often when an employee is not given proper assistance with a personal or company problem, he or she may turn to fellow employees and the problem can become a subject of gossip. Company gossip, if allowed to grow out of bounds, can create internal problems that destroy labor efficiency.

Providing a career ladder will help hold highly motivated employees by giving them the opportunity to move forward in the organization. The less ambitious employee is not likely to become dissatisfied at this so long as it is obvious that the opportunity to go forward is there for all who desire it.

Performance appraisals should be made on a regularly scheduled basis. The appraisal will alert the supervisor and management to people in need of additional training and give them an opportunity to recognize the outstanding worker. Management should strive to keep the performance appraisal impersonal. The appraisal must be done according to a planned procedure and schedule, using standard evaluation methods oriented specifically to the position being appraised.

Staffing and Scheduling

As previously mentioned, classifying personnel and determining the numbers needed in each classification and the hours they are to be employed are largely mechanical functions. The diagram in Exhibit 14–1 (Chapter 14) divides the foodservice operation into major areas. Guided by this diagram and the position classifications developed by the position analyzer, management can determine the staffing necessary at various levels of business activity. The results thus obtained can be put into chart or table form. Two facts are important in making the decisions needed to complete the staffing chart: (1) the amount of time and effort required for each task; and (2) the standard expenditure of effort to be expected of each individual in carrying out his or her duties. Exhibit 15–1 represents a foodservice staffing chart for customer loads ranging from zero to 300 covers per day. Each establishment will have different staffing needs, and since operating methods change as conditions change and as new ideas are adopted (such as convenience foods and modern equipment), the staffing chart must be constantly reviewed and, if necessary, revised.

RESTAURANT STAFFING CHART

Position	Customers		
	0–100	100–200	200–300
Manager	1	1	1
Purchasing Agent	0	1	1
Rec.-Storeroom	1	1	2
Chef	1	1	1
Roast Cook	0	1	1
Fry Cook	0	0	1
Dishwasher—Potwasher	1	2	2
Porter	1	1	2
Waitress Supervisor	1	1	2
Waitress	5	10	15
Busboy	1	2	3
Cashier	0	1	1
Mgr. to assume purchasing	0–100		
Supervisor to cashier	0–100		
Dishwasher to wash pots	0–100		

EXHIBIT 15–1   A hypothetical staffing chart illustrating how personnel requirements can be tabulated on the basis of customer load. Some jobs are combined at low staffing levels.

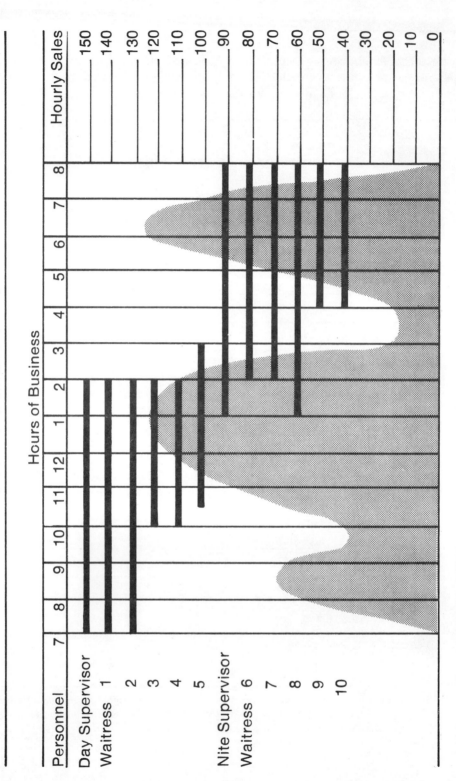

Exhibit Cafe
Personnel Demand Chart

EXHIBIT 15–2 A graph showing how demands for personnel can be plotted as a function of the rise and fall of sales throughout the day, peaking at mealtimes. Staff size and overlapping work periods are shown for a purely hypothetical case.

Exhibit 15–1 is a hypothetical presentation and is used only to show the way in which personnel requirements might be tabulated as a function of business volume. The figures given should not be used for any existing operation. The chart indicates that, at the start of a business, the manager might be able to include menu-making and purchasing in his duties. As business expands it would be necessary to add employees to do these tasks. One waitress or waiter can serve 20 covers, but as the service staff increases with the number of covers served, it will be necessary to increase the amount of dining room supervision. So, for each five servers one supervisor is added. One cook can handle both fry work and roast work up to a certain point. Then it is necessary to hire a specialist for each job. As indicated, some positions are more affected by increases (or decreases) in volume than others. By being alert to requirements as shown by the staffing chart, management can be relatively sure of having the right number of employees available to handle the traffic.

Scheduling may be considered a refinement of staffing. After management has decided on the type and number of employees needed to handle a given volume of business, the personnel should be brought in to match the workload. Accurate records are necessary if employee time is to be used efficiently. Customer count, covers served or dollar volume may be used as the basis for scheduling employees. Of course, we want the most help when volume is high, but it must be remembered that the foodservice business is usually one of peaks and valleys in customer volume. To arrange our labor force to accommodate these high and low points, it may often be necessary to use part-time employees, split shifts and irregular shifts to keep labor costs in line.

Staggering employee working hours so that the beginning hours of one work-shift overlap the ending hours of another at peak periods is good rush-hour strategy, and makes for smooth transition between shifts. The nature of the business at various times of the day affects service requirements. Breakfast, for example, usually requires less service per person, so fewer personnel could be assigned to breakfast than to dinner even if the customer count were the same. Exhibit 15–2 indicates the use of staggered shifts and part-time service employees. The schedule chart should not be taken as a working guide, but as an indication of how this method is used.

Forecasting Personnel Requirements

Charting the relationship between payroll and sales will also facilitate advance planning. Exhibit 15–3 indicates how this may be done. Since business tends to be cyclical in nature, historical payroll figures may be used to budget for sufficient personnel during a given period. Forecasting will allow for an intelligent planning of vacations and permit employees to anticipate lay-off and slack periods. Such a chart will show seasonal effects which may also provide information for decisions on other matters.

Record-Keeping

Keeping of payroll and personnel records is a vital management function not only because the government often requires it, but because important management decisions also depend on these records. A time card or other record should be kept, covering the arrival and departure of each employee. When warranted by the number of employees and the additional supervision required, a time clock should be installed. In large corporations, weekly summaries of all employee time should be maintained by departments. Management often depends on an overall labor cost percentage which may prove to be grossly unfair to some departments. Departmental figures will show which department is coverstaffed or understaffed. Using these figures,

management can spot job problems and take corrective action. From the weekly summary, management should expect to receive explanations of hours worked in excess of those budgeted. Monthly reports should be made, summarizing the weekly reports. Again, overtime and time worked in excess of that allocated in staffing schedules should be explained. Increase or decrease in payroll should be correlated with figures that have been projected for seasonal or peak periods and special events in the budget.

PRODUCTION CONTROLS

Any of the problems discussed in the previous chapter may account for increased labor costs as much as for increases in the cost of food. Diligent production controls are therefore essential.

Menu Planning

Improper menu planning wastes kitchen labor as well as food. Poor planning of the items appearing on the menu (the menu mix) may cause overloading of some preparation areas while other areas are totally ignored. This may mean that some employees are overworked while others are having a difficult time keeping busy. A proper balance in menu items as to the amount of preparation required will keep everyone busy, and help operate the kitchen at peak efficiency.

Hiring unqualified kitchen personnel may be expensive insofar as waste of materials is concerned, but hiring overqualified personnel will be expensive from the viewpoint of labor cost. The menu should suit the type of operation, and kitchen personnel should be hired with regard for their ability to prepare the items called for on the menu. In-

EXHIBIT 15–3   Payroll and sales curves for a downtown restaurant in a non-resort area. In January it took about $200 in payroll to generate $700 in sales. The same costs generated only $550 in October. To make payroll costs conform more closely to receding sales in summer and early autumn, planning for a smaller staff during these months appears to be in order.

creasing the number of items on the menu increases costs in all areas. The more items, the greater the variety of merchandise to be handled, the greater the storage cost, and the slower the service.

Purchasing

Lack of planning and overpurchasing may result in additional handling of foodstuffs at the receiving dock and in the storage area. Allowing shortages to occur because of poor purchasing procedures results in confusion, which can create havoc with labor cost. Adequate and accurate records must be kept if the correct amounts are to be purchased to allow for an orderly production and consumption schedule. Scheduling of hours in which merchandise will be received will provide for the most efficient use of personnel in the receiving area. This will not only ensure having adequately trained personnel on hand to receive all merchandise properly, but will also allow receiving personnel to be scheduled for other duties as needed. Purchasing in quantities that have been carefully planned by using consumption rates established from accounting records, limiting receiving hours, and controlling storeroom issuing hours will develop efficiency and hold payroll expense for these tasks to a minimum.

Service

The amount of service required will vary with the kind of food, the style of service and a host of other factors. Formal dining room service will require more personnel than informal buffet, luncheon, or snack-food service. The importance of record-keeping in planning the size of the service staff can hardly be overemphasized. Daily and hourly records are normally required, and occasionally data for even smaller segments of time should be recorded (see Exhibits 14–10, 14–11 and 14–12 in Chapter 14). It must be remembered that the food-service organization is buying hours of employee time and these hours of service should be purchased with the same consideration as one would buy any other commodity.

Clientele

The more formal the service and the more demanding the clientele the more difficult becomes the problem of controlling labor cost. For this reason the controls will be more closely studied and enforced when the number of employees and complexity of service is increased. Clientele demands cannot always be offset by menu price increases sufficient to cover the additional cost. When these demands can no longer be met on a profitable basis, a management decision is in order, and this will normally take the form of curtailment in personnel, simplification of the service, a radical price change, or some combination of these measures.

Hours of Operation

Extending hours of operation does not always generate sufficient income to offset the expense incurred. Management must determine what hours are right for the particular operation. It is for this reason there are foodservices operating 24 hours a day while others are open for only one meal. The management tool described in Chapter 8 of this text—the break-even analysis—will help determine

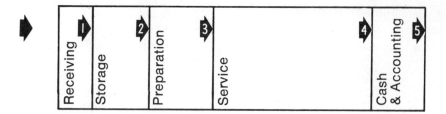

EXHIBIT 15–4   The flow of merchandise. A facilities layout that channels work "downstream" will inevitably promote labor efficiency.

when it is more profitable to close than to be open. In respect to hours of operation, the scheduling chart offered as Exhibit 15–2 will be helpful. It is usually found that when too many employees are available for the amount of business present, not only labor costs rise but general efficiency suffers.

Layout and Design

The layout and design of the entire operation is of utmost importance in the control of labor costs. The kitchen must be designed to facilitate preparation of the food called for by the menu. The service area must be designed to produce the greatest efficiency consistent with the aesthetic scheme of the interior decorator. The basic plan for any foodservice organization can be visualized in terms of how it permits the flow of merchandise from receipt of the raw product to consumption of the finished product by the guest. Laying out the various areas to conform to this "flow" and locating these areas so that they serve as units in one harmonious system will provide a built-in capability for controlling labor costs. Exhibit 15–4 indicates the flow described. The importance of time-and-motion studies, layout and design, and their relationship to the personnel prob-

lem is graphically presented in Exhibit 15–5, which examines the cost of walking (on the job), and Exhibit 15–6, which illustrates how plan design can save "mileage" and reduce costs. These two

HOW MUCH ARE YOU PAYING FOR WALKING?

Pay of Employee per Week	Labor Cost of 10 Paces (25 feet)	Walking Distance that Costs 1¢ (for each pay level)
Walking Cost under Load		
$ 35	0.6¢	42 feet
50	.9	28
60	1.0	25
70	1.2	21
80	1.4	18
90	1.6	16
100	1.7	15
Walking Cost without Load		
$ 35	0.4¢	57 feet
50	.6	40
60	.8	33
70	.9	29
80	1.0	25
90	1.1	22
100	1.3	20

Source: Adapted from Michigan State University Extension Service publication presenting U. S. Bureau of Standards labor costs data.

EXHIBIT 15–5   Some data on what it costs to walk—on company time.

HOW FAR DOES YOUR WAITRESS WALK?

RESTAURANT NO I

RESTAURANT NO II

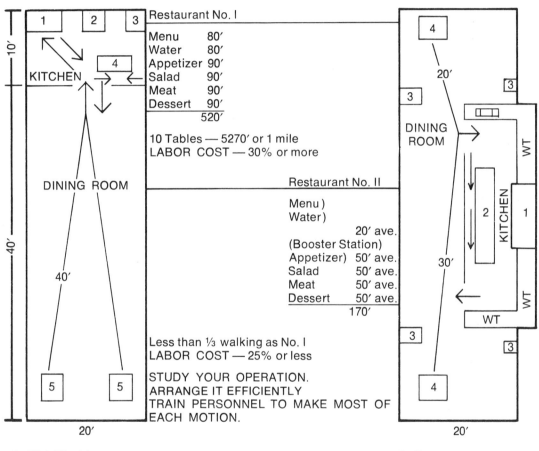

Restaurant No. I

Menu	80'
Water	80'
Appetizer	90'
Salad	90'
Meat	90'
Dessert	90'
	520'

10 Tables — 5270' or 1 mile
LABOR COST — 30% or more

Restaurant No. II

Menu)
Water)
        20' ave.
(Booster Station)
Appetizer) 50' ave.
Salad   50' ave.
Meat   50' ave.
Dessert   50' ave.
          170'

Less than 1/3 walking as No. I
LABOR COST — 25% or less

STUDY YOUR OPERATION.
ARRANGE IT EFFICIENTLY
TRAIN PERSONNEL TO MAKE MOST OF
EACH MOTION.

1. Dish Washing
2. Table
3. Range
4. Serving Table
5. Guests

1. Ranges
2. Serving Table
3. Booster Stations
4. Guests

EXHIBIT 15–6   How placement of facilities affects "travel time" of the service staff. (Adapted from Michigan State University Extension Service publication presenting U.S. Bureau of Standards labor-costs data.)

studies were developed by the U.S. Bureau of Standards. They show the influence of layout and design on the number of employees hired and on the efficiency of the labor force.

SUMMARY

The cost of labor in a foodservice is one of the two major expenses in the operation. It is a cost over which management has some measure of control. Management's responsibility in determining personnel policy involves all the relationships between the foodservice company and the individual, and also the relationships between individuals that develop within the foodservice operation.

To be able to specify the kind of person needed for a given position—in other words, to establish job specifications—one must be able to describe the job accurately and completely and this requires careful analysis of the work involved. The job specification is an essential step in the process of recruiting the right individual.

There is no one source from which all employees can be recruited. The degree of skill and education required for a position in some degree determines the media used to find the employee desired. Selection of employees should be based on as wide a choice as possible.

Employee orientation, training, counseling, career ladders and performance appraisals are all important if we are to keep good employees on the job and get them to produce at peak efficiency.

Staffing and scheduling are mechanical activities requiring a large accumulation of data and effective use of it. Staffing and scheduling charts can be valuable guides in making the most efficient use of labor. Staffing and scheduling should be the culmination of systematic and informed decision-making, and should be carried out as objectively as possible. Leadership and morale are vital but distinct management responsibilities.

An overall payroll cost percentage may be used as a guide, but for greatest efficiency and control, staffing and scheduling should be done by department.

STUDY QUESTIONS

1. Name three of the principal factors influencing labor costs in a foodservice establishment, and discuss briefly.
2. Describe the manager's responsibility with respect to the preparation of job specifications.
3. What are the major steps in the recruitment process?
4. Why is it considered unwise to hire a person who is overqualified for the job? Explain how you would avoid this recruiting pitfall.
5. Discuss the value of employee orientation and training as a means of reducing labor costs.

6. What use is made of payroll and personnel records in staffing and scheduling? Describe briefly how a staffing chart is constructed.

7. Illustrate with a simple sketch how staggering employee working hours helps to handle periods of peak business activity.

8. Consider the effects of menu planning on labor costs, and cite a typical case in which a particular menu item might increase labor as well as food costs.

Bibliography

Bauer, Royal D. M., and Paul H. Darby. *Elementary Accounting.* New York: Barnes and Noble, 1970.

Blecke, Curtis J. *Financial Analysis for Decision-Making.* Englewood Cliffs, N.J.: Prentice-Hall, 1966.

Brodner, Joseph, Howard M. Carlson, and Henry T. Maschal. *Profitable Food and Beverage Operation.* 4th revised edition. New York: Ahrens Book Company, 1962.

Davidson, Sidney, James S. Schindler, and Roman L. Weil. *Accounting: The Language of Business.* Glen Ridge, N.J.: Thomas Horton and Daughters, 1974.

Dukas, Peter, and Donald E. Lundberg. *How to Operate a Restaurant.* New York: Ahrens Publishing Co., 1963.

Elliott, Travis. A series of manuals entitled *Profitable Food Service Management thru* (subjects 1–9). Chicago: National Restaurant Association, 1966.

Fay, Clifford T., Jr., Richard Rhoads, and Robert Rosenblatt. *Managerial Accounting for the Hospitality Service Industries.* Dubuque, Iowa: Wm. C. Brown Company, 1971.

Fertig, Paul E., Donald F. Istvan, and Homer J. Mottice. *Using Accounting Information.* 2nd edition. New York: Harcourt Brace Jovanovich, 1971.

Foulke, R. A. *Practical Financial Statement Analysis.* 5th edition. New York: McGraw-Hill, 1961.

Horwath, Ernest B., Louis Toth, and J. D. LeSure. *Hotel Accounting.* 3rd edition. New York: Ronald Press, 1963.

Laventhol Krekstein Horwath & Horwath. *Uniform System of Accounts for Restaurants.* 4th revised edition. Chicago: National Restaurant Association, 1968.

Lynch, Richard M. *Accounting for Management: Planning & Control.* New York: McGraw-Hill, 1967.

Matz, Adolph, Othel J. Curry, and George W. Frank. *Cost Accounting.* 3rd edition. Cincinnati: South-Western Publishing Company, 1962.

Michigan State University Cooperative Extension Service, "Management Through Figures (in the Lodging Industry)," Bulletin 565, Sept. 1969.

Moore, Carl L., and Robert K. Jaedicke. *Managerial Accounting.* 3rd edition. Cincinnati: South-Western Publishing Company, 1972.

Myer, John N. *Accounting for Non-Accountants.* New York: Hawthorn Books, 1967.

Pritchard, Leland J. *Money and Banking.* 2nd edition. Boston: Houghton Mifflin, 1964.

Radigan, J. Terry. *A Financial Analysis of the Restaurant Industry.* Chicago: National Restaurant Association, 1963.

University of Massachusetts Cooperative Extension Service.
Leaflet 11, "Using Financial State-ments in Food Service Establish-ments," 1964.
Leaflet 12, "Operating Budgets for Food Service Establishments," 1967.
Leaflet 13, "Using Break-Even Anal-ysis in Food Service Establish-ments," 1967.

Glossary

At best a glossary simplifies the meaning of a word, favoring a special connotation; at worst it coddles and misleads the reader. This glossary is no more than a quick-and-easy reference for the terms used in this book. For definitive meanings refer to discussions in the text.

Account　A record of the status of an asset, liability, revenue, expense, etc.

Accounting equation　Assets = Liabilities + Capital.

Accounting period　The time-period covered by an operating statement; fiscal period.

Account payable　Amount owed to a creditor; a debt; a liability.

Account receivable　Amount due from a customer or other debtor; an asset.

Accrual accounting　Accounting method whereby entries are made on the basis of when goods and services are rendered.

Accrue　To grow, accumulate.

Acid-test ratio　(See **Quick ratio.**)

Amortize　To extinguish gradually, as an asset or debt.

Asset　Property or resource owned by the business.

Audit　A verification of accounting records.

Balance　The difference remaining between debits and credits in an account—a debit balance if positive, a credit balance if negative.

Balance sheet　Statement showing that assets equal liabilities plus capital. (Also called a statement of financial position.)

Bond　A certificate of debt, as one binding a corporation to repay money with interest, and on a date, specified.

Break-even point　That point on the graph of business operations indicating the sales level at which revenues and costs are equal and there is neither profit nor loss.

Budget　A business plan expressed in monetary terms, projecting sales and costs.

Business entity　A business establishment treated as a separate "individual" for accounting purposes.

Capital　The original investment in a business plus accumulated profits; total assets less liabilities. (Also called net worth and owner's equity.) As a general economic term, wealth used to create wealth.

Capital stock　Ownership shares of a corporation. (See **Common stock** and **Preferred stock.**)

Cash　Coin or currency; and any instrument readily convertible into money—bank check, money order, etc.

Cash accounting　Accounting method whereby entries are made on the basis of when goods and services are paid for.

Cash statement   Abbreviated term for the **Statement of changes in financial position** (see).

Collateral   Assets pledged by the borrower as additional security for a loan.

Common statement   A financial statement giving data in percentages.

Common stock   Stock issued to participating owners of a corporation whose claims on the assets and earnings give way to payment of debts and prescribed dividends to holders of preferred stock, but whose interests are thereafter unlimited.

Consistency   The accounting principle calling for use of the same methods from period to period in handling like transactions.

Corporation   A body of associated persons given the legal status of an individual and authorized to operate for commercial, or other, purposes in accordance with a charter approved by the state.

Cost   The value of an asset not yet converted or consumed in producing income. Informally used to mean the price at which goods and services are acquired, and often used as a synonym for **Expense** (see).

Cost of sales   Cost of goods sold.

Cover   Place setting, especially for one person; a unit in establishing customer count.

Credit   Right-hand entry in an account.

Creditor   A lender, or other entity to which the company is liable for a debt.

Creditor's equity   Liability; right of a creditor to assets.

Current assets   Cash, or other assets to be converted into cash within a year.

Current ratio   Ratio of current assets to current liabilities.

Debit   Left-hand entry in an account.

Deficit   Generally, a deficiency in income; specifically, a debit balance in the retained earnings account.

Depreciation   Systematic write-off of the value (cost) of a fixed asset.

Double-entry accounting   Accounting system in which equal debit and credit entries are made for each transaction, keeping the accounting equation in balance.

Earnings   Income; total profits for a period.

Equity   A right; claim on assets.

Expenditure   A disbursement of funds, or an incurrence of a liability, for goods or service.

Expense   The cost of assets consumed or converted in generating income; an expired cost.

Financial position   The condition of a business in terms of its assets and equities, as stated on the balance sheet.

Fiscal year   Annual accounting period; financial year. (Often different from the regular calendar twelve-month.)

Fixed assets   Assets used over a period of years, as land, building, equipment; plant assets.

Fixed budget   Budget based on a single sales projection.

Fixed costs   Basic costs of being in business, unaffected by the volume of business; costs of plant, insurance, taxes, etc.

Flexible budget   Budget based on two or more possible levels of sales activity.

Foodservice Industry term denoting commercial and institutional food preparation and service or the establishments so engaged.

Franchise The right or privilege to use the name and products of another under a legal grant; the financial and operational system establishing such rights; the enterprise so established.

Full disclosure True and complete presentation of information material to the financial state of a business.

Going concern Business entity with a future; the fundamental accounting assumption that a business will remain in operation indefinitely.

Goodwill Estimable earning power of a business beyond the fair market value of tangible assets; value of its name or reputation.

Gross profit Net sales less cost of goods sold.

Historical cost Original, acquisition cost, unadjusted for current values.

Income Exchange value of goods or services in the primary operations of a business; excess of revenue over expense.

Income & expense statement Financial summary of business operations for a specified period. (Also called profit and loss statement.)

Inventory Assets in the form of raw materials, work in process, and supplies on hand. As a verb, to cite and compute the cost of such stores.

Journal Summary of daily transactions as they occur; book of original entry.

Ledger A book of accounts to which entries in the journal are posted.

Legal entity A state-of-being recognized by law, as that of a business or other corporation which has the rights and liabilities of an individual; a business entity with legal status.

Leverage A measure of the relationship between owners' equity and creditors' equity; the extent to which others' money is being used to generate income.

Liability A debt or obligation to a creditor; creditor's equity.

Liquidation Payment of debt; especially, sale of assets in settlement of debts on the occasion of closing down the business.

Liquidity The strength of a business in terms of its working capital, or the ability to pay debts as they come due.

Loss Excess of cost over revenue; negative income.

Matching Relating expense to the income it was instrumental in earning; recognizing associated income and expense in the same period.

Mean The average value of a group of numbers (arithmetic mean); the sum of two or more quantities divided by the number of quantities.

Median The middle point in a series of numbers; the number which has half the numbers of a series below it in value, and half above it.

Mortgage A claim against property which the borrower gives to the lender to secure a loan. (Popularly used in reference to the loan so secured.) A chattel mortgage is a mortgage on personal property.

Net assets   Total assets minus total liabilities. (Also called owner's equity, capital, and net worth.)

Net worth   (See **Capital**.)

Note payable   A liability evidenced by a written promise to pay at a specified time.

Note receivable   An asset evidenced by a promissory note from the borrower.

Open account   An account with a debit or credit balance.

Owner's equity   Assets to which an owner has the right. (See **Capital**.)

Partnership   An unincorporated business owned by two or more individuals.

Periodicity   Frequency of an evolution or event, said of recurrent statements, budgets, inventories, inspections, etc., covering specified operating periods.

Posting   Transferring journal entries to their corresponding ledger accounts.

Preferred stock   Ownership stock with prior claim to dividends over common stock, but deferring to claims of bondholders and payment of other debt; stock issued to shareholders with nonvoting interest in a corporation.

Prepaid expense   Advance payment, as for rent or insurance, accounted for as an asset until the benefit period is past, when the item is expensed.

Prime cost   Total of all costs assigned directly to a product; in a foodservice, the combined cost of food and labor.

Profit   Excess of income over expense for a transaction (also called *net profit* as distinguished from *gross profit*). (Multiple profits for a period are *earnings*.)

Profit & loss statement   (See **Income & expense statement**.)

Pro forma   As a formality, perfunctorily (said of an invoice or financial statement giving the form of the document but containing hypothetical or tentative figures).

Proprietorship   An unincorporated business owned by a single individual; sole ownership; also, a general term for ownership.

Quick assets   Cash plus readily convertible securities and receivables.

Quick ratio   Ratio of quick assets to current liabilities. (Also called the acid-test ratio.)

Retained earnings   Net income added to the capital of a corporation, since its beginning, after payment of dividends to stockholders; owners' equity less paid-in capital.

Revenue   The exchange value of goods sold or services rendered in the primary operations of a business.

Sale   A revenue transaction (capital account) involving delivery of goods or service for cash or for an obligation to pay.

Securities   Documents witnessing ownership or indebtedness, such as stock certificates, bonds, and similar instruments.

Single-entry bookkeeping   Simple, cash bookkeeping on a revenue-expense basis, not self-balancing.

Solvency   Ability to meet current obligations.

Statement of changes in financial position   Statement explaining changes in working capital (or cash) during a specified period. (Abbreviated as *cash statement* in this text.)

Statement of financial position   (See **Balance sheet**.)

T-account   Conventional account form in shape of T, with title across the top, debits to the left of the vertical line, credits to the right.

Transaction   Business event resulting in an accounting entry.

Trial balance   A totaling of all debit balances and credit balances to establish their equality, and as a check on the completeness and accuracy of accounting entries.

Turnover   The frequency of change in assets, as in the inventory of a foodservice, during an operating period; an activity ratio.

Variable budget   (See **Flexible budget**.)

Variable costs   Costs which vary with the volume of business; for example, the cost of food, additional labor and incidental expenses as more customers are served.

Working capital   Funds remaining after current liabilities are deducted from current assets.

Working capital ratio   Ratio of net sales to net working capital.

Index